Quilted Postcards

'Little Quilts Of Creativity'

By Sarah Sparkes

www.tortoisecrafts.co.uk

Editing Tony Sparkes

Proof reading Laura Sparkes

Published by Tortoise Crafts Publishing
All enquiries to: editor@tortoisecraftspublishing.co.uk

First Edition

First published 2020

ISBN: 978-1-8380342-0-7

Dedication

To my husband, Tony, who made this possible.

To our daughter, Laura, for all the help.

And to my best friend, Rachel, for all the encouragement over the years.

Thank you.

Sarah

Contents

Introduction

For years my husband and daughter have been telling me that I should share my Quilted Postcards with more people than those I send them to. A few years ago, I sat down and made a list of postcards that I thought could work in a book and we've gone from there. This book contains 16 basic postcards and a multitude of possible variations for you to make. Each postcard has been given a level of difficulty – easy, intermediate, expert – to make it easier for you to work through them.

What is a Quilted Postcard?

A Quilted Postcard is a 4"x 6" piece of fabric art made using three layers. The size makes it a postcard and the three layers make it a quilt. They are a lot quicker to make than a traditionally sized quilt and are perfect to be given as gifts to someone or to be mounted on a card and sent for special occasions such as Birthday, Anniversary, Christmas, Easter, New Baby, New Home. The limit really is your imagination.

How to use this book

The first Postcard, Tree in a Tub, has detailed instructions needed to make the basic Quilted Postcards and I recommend that you start there before making any of the other Postcards in this book. The instructions for the other Postcards only include instructions specific to that postcard. Throughout this book you will find , my logo. She marks where I give my personal hints and tips to help you make your postcards.

Happy Creating!

Sarah

Basic Supplies

These are what I use but you can use whatever you find works best for you

Fabrics

As I am a patchwork quilter I have a huge range of 100% cotton fabric and it is these that I use for most of my Quilted Postcards. Cotton is easier to work with and comes in a huge range of colours and patterns.

For the back of the postcard I use a white cotton fabric. I buy a better quality bleached calico (USA muslin) for this.

Threads

I use a big range of threads on my Sewing Machine. I have lots of thread in my workroom and I use whichever works best with the current project - from standard sewing cotton, sew-all to rayons for embroidery and machine quilting threads - from plains to variegated threads.

Stranded Embroidery Cotton

I use DMC, and as I also do cross stitch, and so does my daughter, we have boxes and boxes of threads. If you don't have any then I would recommend buying a few of the variegated ones, as they have light and dark colours in.

Iron on interfacing

Again use the product that you prefer, as long as it is white, medium weight and iron-on. Follow the manufacturers instructions for pressing the interfacing onto the fabric.

Wadding

All the wadding that I use is leftovers/offcuts from my patchwork quilting. As I prefer to use Hobbs Heirloom (80/20) for this, it is also used in the postcards. I would recommend a wadding that doesn't mind pressing, so not a polyester one.

Fusible Web

Use your favourite one, mine is Vlieseline Wonderweb, I buy a big box of it as I do go through a lot! Wonderweb is a paper backed sheet of thin glue. Designs are marked on the paper side and cut out with an allowance all round. With the paper side upmost it is laid onto the wrong size of the fabric being used and pressed into place with an iron to melt the glue onto the fabric. The shape is then cut out to the line, paper peeled off, and placed glue side down onto the background fabric. It's then again pressed with the iron to melt the glue and attach the shape to the background fabric ready to be stitched. Please follow the manufactures recommended iron temperature for the fusible web being used.

Sewing Machine

Although a sewing machine isn't essential for creating Quilted Postcards it does make them quicker and easier to do, especially finishing the edges. Every sewing machine is different, you know your machine best and the stitches it does and the best threads for it.

I use just three stitches to create the Postcards, straight, zig zag and blanket (applique) stitch.

I also prefer to use my walking foot (Even feed foot).

I guess I should tell you that I use Bernina Sewing Machines, the one I use mostly is an Aurora 440QE. I also have two others, one I take to classes, Activa 135 and my original 1130 that I bought over thirty years ago. The only thing I learnt in school sewing lessons was that Bernina sewing machines were really good and could cope with thirty girls attempting to sew, all the other machines broke down!

Marking Pencils and Pens

I use a normal pencil for a lot of the marking, please check that whichever pencil you use for drawing on the fusible web, doesn't come off onto the iron, as it is really annoying to find that you have ruined a piece of fabric because the pencil has come off onto it - especially a pale colour.

For marking on details to be embroidered I use Clover Air erasable pen and occasionally for white or very pale fabric a Frixion pen, but these tend to leave a white line on darker fabrics when pressed.

For writing on the back of the postcards and sometimes other bits I use a Pigma Micron Archival Ink black No.3.

Odif 505 Temporary Adhesive spray

This is optional but I find it useful.

Rotary Cutter, Self-healing Mat and Rulers

If you have them then use them, if you haven't then scissors are just as good. I have a big range of different sizes and makes of rulers, use the ones that you are most comfortable with for the size of the project. I mostly for postcard making use my 6" square ruler and my 1" x 14" ruler. Both are designed to be non-slip but with all my rulers I add extra non-slip discs (by TrueGrip) and I find that they 'hold' onto the fabric even more and are less likely to move.

Iron and Ironing Mat

Whatever you usually use. I have an iron and ironing mat that are only used for patchwork, as no matter how careful you are, accidents happen and fusible web or interfacing will get stuck to the iron or ironing mat! My ironing mat has a removable cover, made from a brushed cotton cot sheet (from when our daughter was a baby!) that I take off regularly and throw in the towel wash and any fusible web or other stuff that has accidently got stuck to it comes off.

Scissors

My preferred scissors are my Fiskars embroidery and Fiskars General purpose 16.5cm ones, these get used for everything!!! I know scissors should only be used for fabric, but I use these for fabric, fusible web and paper. I find them a nice size and weight.

Hand sewing needles, thimble, and pins

Whatever you find best and prefer.

Colle Temporaire
pour tissu
Temporary Adhesive
for fabric
Temporärer Kleber
für Stoff
MICRON 03
Luftlöslicher Vorzeichenstift
Dick
QUILT-N-SEW RULER

Starter Postcard—Tree In A Tub

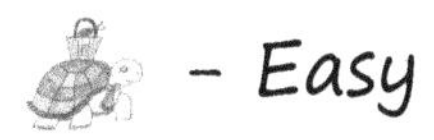 - Easy

This is the first postcard to try. I give you all the basic information to make not only this postcard but the other postcards in this book as well. So please, make this first as it will make creating the others a lot easier.

It is a postcard that is ideal for Birthday's, Thank You or just saying 'Hello'. As the title says, it is a 'Tree In A Tub'!

You will need to make this postcard

- 2 pieces of white cotton fabric 4½" x 6½"
- 2 pieces of iron-on interfacing 4½" x 6½"
- 1 piece of wadding 4" x 6"
- Fusible web
- A selection of fabrics
- A selection of sewing threads
- A selection of stranded embroidery cottons

1) Take the fabric for the background and draw a 4" x 6" (postcard size) rectangle onto the right side of the fabric cut out with a ¼" allowance all around.

Rather than constantly having to measure my postcards, I have a piece of card cut to 4" x 6". With this I can check a piece of fabric is big enough to make a postcard and also quickly mark the size, without having to measure.

2) Press one of the pieces of interfacing onto the wrong side of the background fabric.

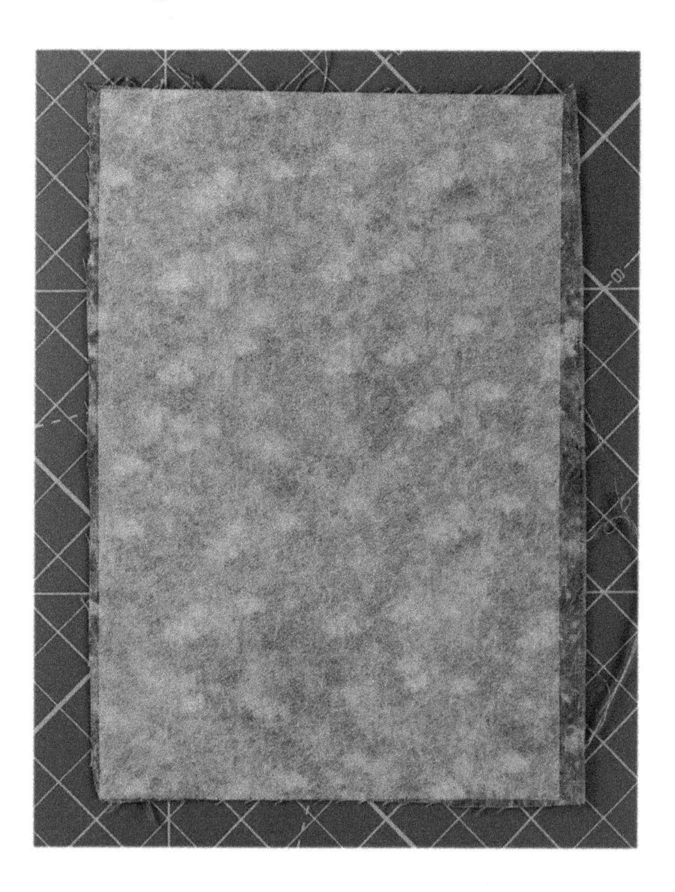

3) Take your fusible web and place – paper side up – on top of the template. Trace on the design.

4) Cut out the traced design with a ¼" extra all round.

All my designs included in this book are hand drawn and so are a bit quirky, it's how I create patterns. They are also the correct size and way round for just putting fusible web on top and tracing the design straight on, without enlarging etc!

5) Take your fabric for the tub and tree and press the fusible web pieces onto the wrong side of the chosen fabrics with the iron.

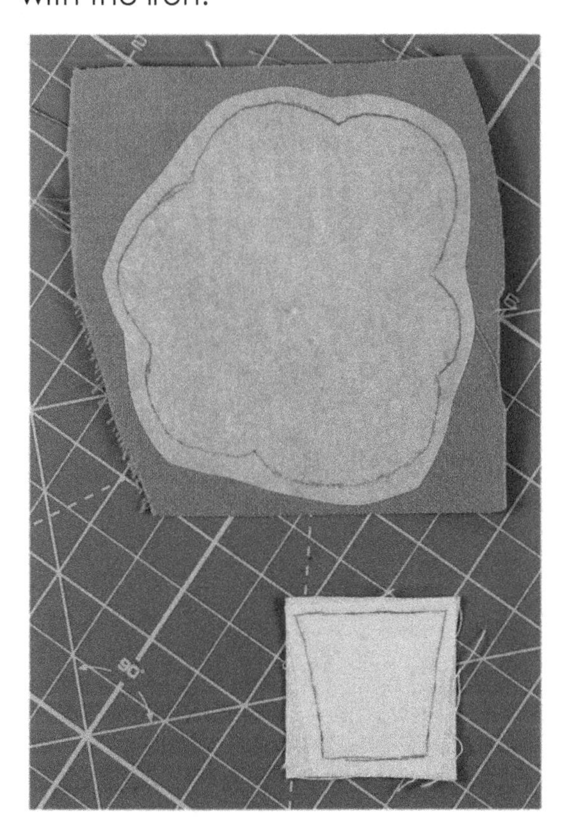

6) Cut out the design pieces on the marked line.

7) Peel off the backing paper and position in place on the background of the postcard, using a ruler to get level and central. Press carefully in place with the iron.

I find it really useful to have a bowl or small bin beside me to keep my workplace tidy and throw the waste in it. Mine are a plastic 'Winnie the Pooh' bowl from when my daughter was a baby, and a pink plastic one called 'Fred'.

8) Layer with the wadding and a piece of white cotton fabric.

I use the 505 temporary spray adhesive to hold the layers together. If you are using this, please remember to spray it on the wadding and only in small amounts.

9) Using your preferred stitches and sewing thread, stitch round the tree. Please remember to pull the threads to the back and knot off the threads. Then trim close to the knots. This is for all thread ends.

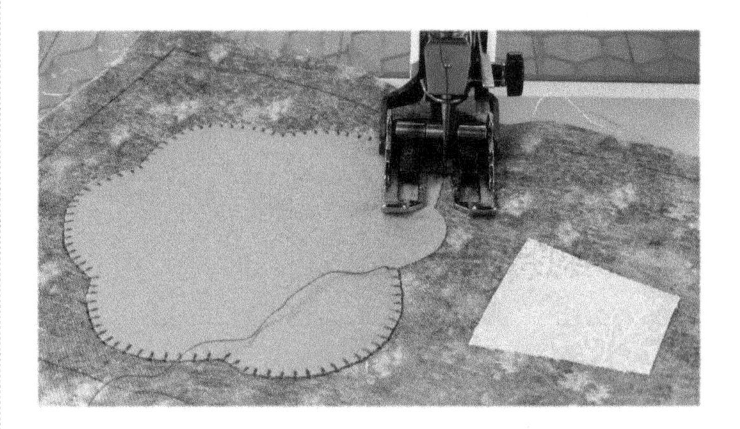

I have used blanket stitch and green thread.

10) Stitch round the tub.

I have used a narrow zig-zag stitch and pink thread. On my sewing machine the size of stitch is 0.4 x 2.4. However I know not all machines can be adjusted the same as mine.

11) Mark on the trunk and branches for the hand embroidery with an air erasable pen.

I draw them on freehand, but I know some people have problems with this. You can use dressmakers' carbon and a mirror image of the pattern to draw the details on.

12) Start by hand embroidering the trunk and branches.

I use two strands of embroidery cotton and split stitch. All embroidery instructions are at the back of the book. Embroidering through the postcard is a bit harder than normal embroidery as you are working through a number of layers, so it might be as well to try different needles until you find the one you are comfortable using. I actually use a quilting needle.

13) Embroider the leaves.

The leaves are stitched in lazy daisy stitch, again using two strands of embroidery cotton.

14) Take the other piece of white fabric and press the other piece of interfacing onto the back. Pin this to the back of the postcard, making sure the white cotton is on the outside. This will make the back of the postcard where you can write your message.

15) Stitch round the postcard, just inside the marked line, using zig-zag stitch and the green thread used for the tree.

I use the standard setting for zig-zag for my machine – 1.5 x 3.3.

16) If you are using a rotary cutter and ruler and mat, place your postcard on the mat – ruler along the marked line – and cut the excess fabric off. This can be done using a pair of scissors if you do not have a rotary cutter.

17) Zig-zag round the postcard again with a slightly closer and wider stitch.

I use 0.9 x 3.6 for the second pass.

18) Using a pair of scissors, trim off the 'fluffy' bits on the edges and the ends of threads.

19) Go round the edge for the third time.

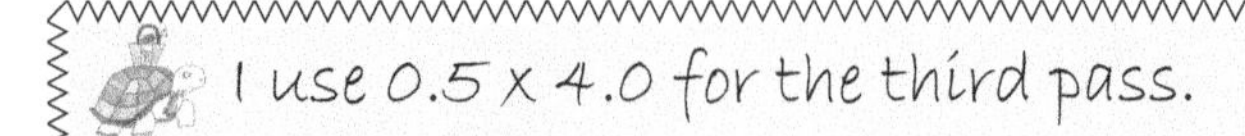

20) Trim the 'fluffy' bits off again.

21) Stitch round the postcard for the final time.

I use 0.4 x 4.2. This creates a nice dense finishing edge. If you are hand stitching this you would need to bind the edge as you would a quilt or wall hanging.

22) Trim the 'fluffy' bits off for the final time.

23) Turn to the back of the postcard and add any decoration that you wish.

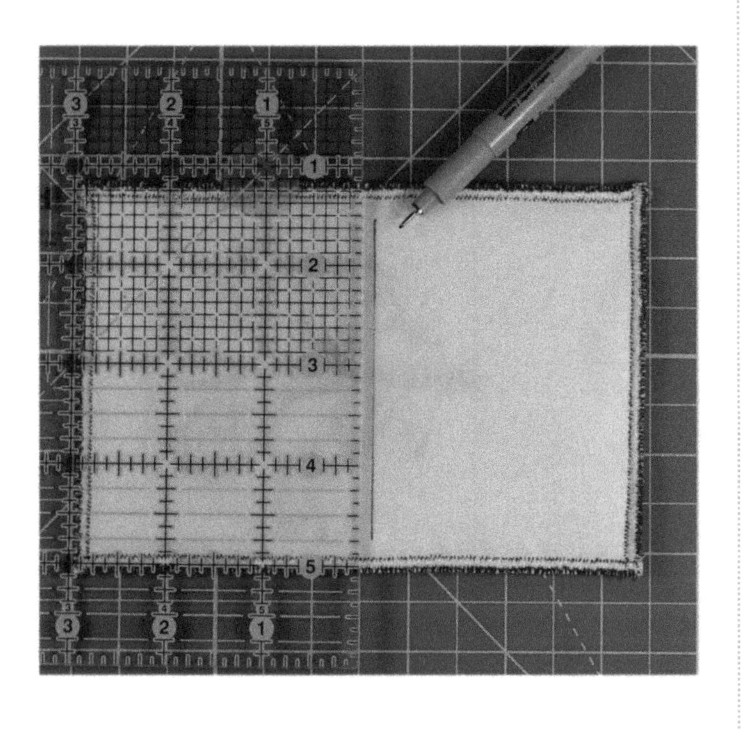

For mine I imitate 'real' postcards. The centre line is drawn using a ruler and Pigma Micron pen. I then stamp my "makers" mark underneath the centre line and create the postage stamp with a stamp of my logo – both using rubber stamps and VersaCraft black ink. Using the Pigma Micron pen, I draw the outside of the postage stamp and the franking mark. The franking mark is drawn using a Guttermann 100m empty cotton reel as this is the perfect size. Inside the franking mark I write the date the postcard was made.

Template for Tree In A Tub

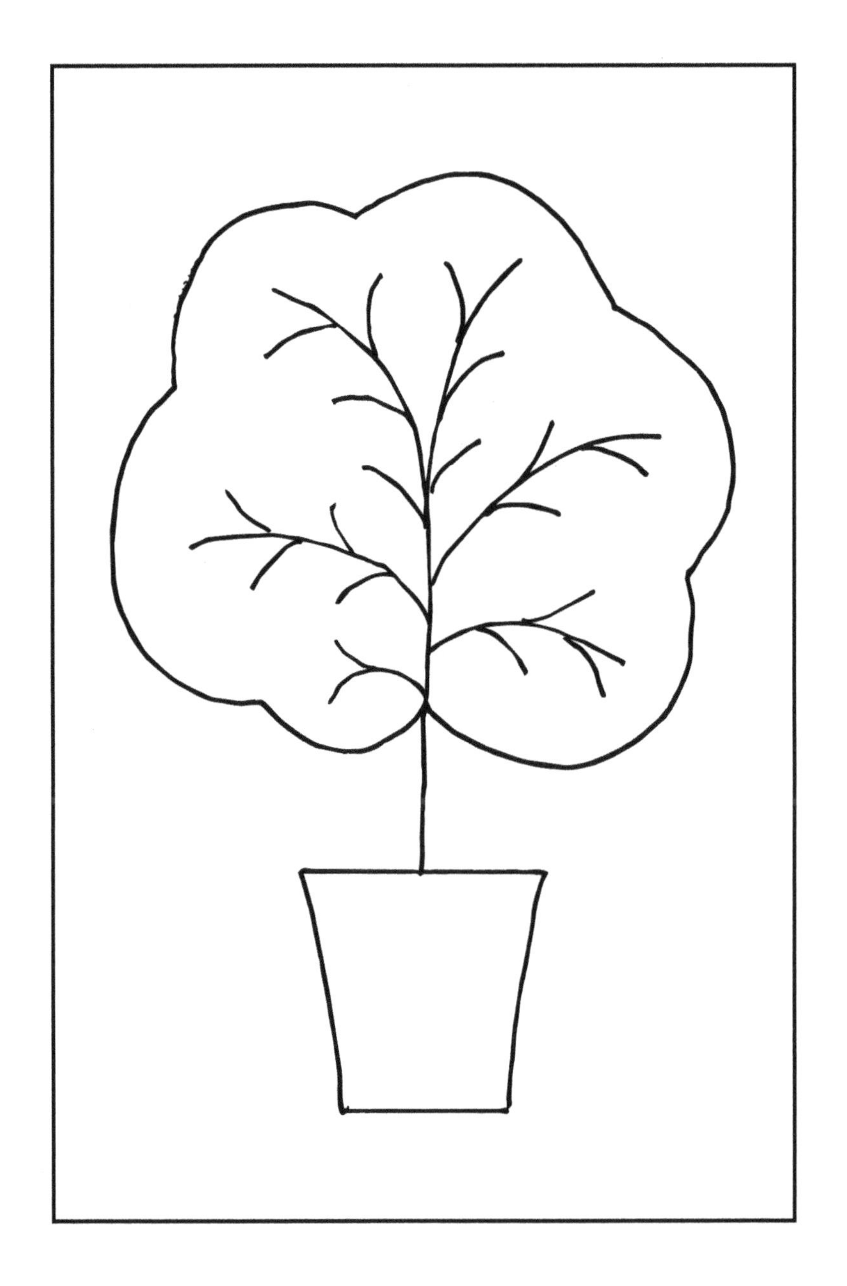

Just a reminder, all you need to do is to lay the fusible web paper side up onto this template and draw on the tub and tree.

This version is the same design, but created in different colours.

For this version I have used 'Spring' colours and a plain background. I have embroidered more leaves and added French knots in one strand of white, and one of pink, to make the blossom. I've also added French knots on the top of the pot.

Love

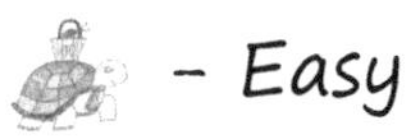

This range of Quilted Postcards are for all those occasions when you want to say I love you, Happy Anniversary, Happy Valentines or for a wedding postcard.

You will need to make this postcard

- 2 pieces of white cotton fabric 4½" x 6½"
- 2 pieces of iron-on interfacing 4½" x 6½"
- 1 piece of wadding 4" x 6"
- Fusible web
- A selection of fabrics
- A selection of sewing threads

1) Draw the two hearts onto the paper side of the fusible web and cut out with a ¼" extra all round.

2) Press onto the chosen fabrics and cut out on the line.

3) Press the design pieces onto the prepared background fabric.

4) Layer with the wadding and rectangle of white fabric.

5) Machine stitch the design.

6) Quilt inside each heart and then around the outside of the hearts on the background fabric.

7) Pin the stabilised white fabric rectangle on the back and stitch around a number of times.

Use just one heart in the centre of the postcard and then stitch the word 'Love' across.

I use a children's plastic stencil for the words as they are really the simplest way of transferring letters on-to fabric and they come in a range of sizes and are inexpensive, a great tool to have.

This postcard just has the rose – in yellow for a Golden wedding anniversary, but it works in any colour.

Because I used the whole template for the leaves, they show through under the rose.

This is a bit more complicated to make, just one heart and the rose. The shape of the petals are quilted onto the rose.

For the rose, draw on the design free hand and then, when stitching, start in the middle and work outwards. I have used a very narrow zig-zag but it also looks good in a heavier thread and straight stitch.

Template for Love

Just a reminder, all you need to do is to lay the fusible web paper side up onto this template and draw on the hearts.

Template for Love Variations

You can use all or some of the above templates to make the various different Love designs. I do not always use the full template if it is hidden by another, as it can show through depending on the colour of the fabric used.

Cupcake

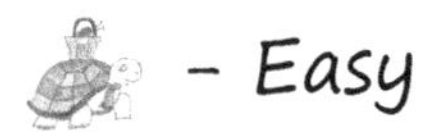 - Easy

This is a simple postcard – and who doesn't like a cupcake! And this one doesn't put any weight on!!!! From the basic design this postcard can be changed and added to in so many ways. It is a postcard that is ideal for birthdays, especially the 'big' number ones and even for a Christmas postcard.

For inspiration just look in any cupcake cookbook.

You will need to make this postcard

- 2 pieces of white cotton fabric 4½" x 6½"
- 2 pieces of iron-on interfacing 4½" x 6½"
- 1 piece of wadding 4" x 6"
- Fusible web
- A selection of fabrics
- A selection of sewing threads
- A selection of beads
- Black Micron Pigma pen

1) Draw the pattern pieces, Cupcake, Icing and the Candle, onto the paper side of the fusible web and cut out with a ¼" extra all round.

2) Press onto the chosen fabrics and cut out on the line.

3) Press the design pieces onto the prepared background fabric.

4) Layer with the wadding and rectangle of white fabric.

5) Machine stitch the design.

6) On the cupcake case stitch lines up the case to make it look like the folds in a paper case.

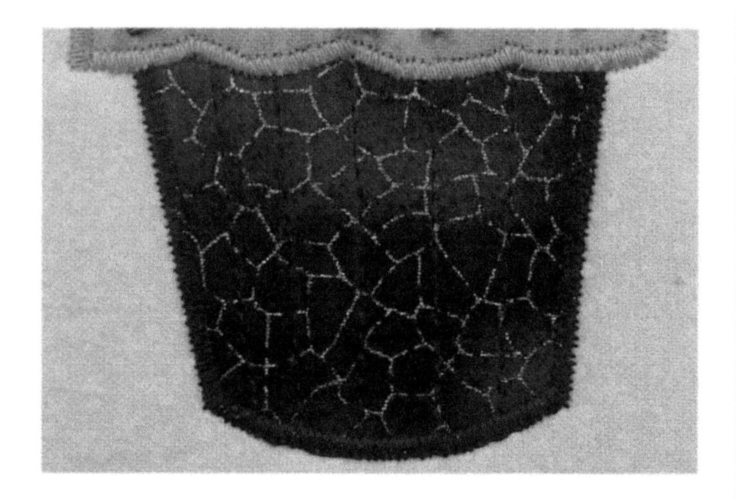

7) Stitch the beads in place.

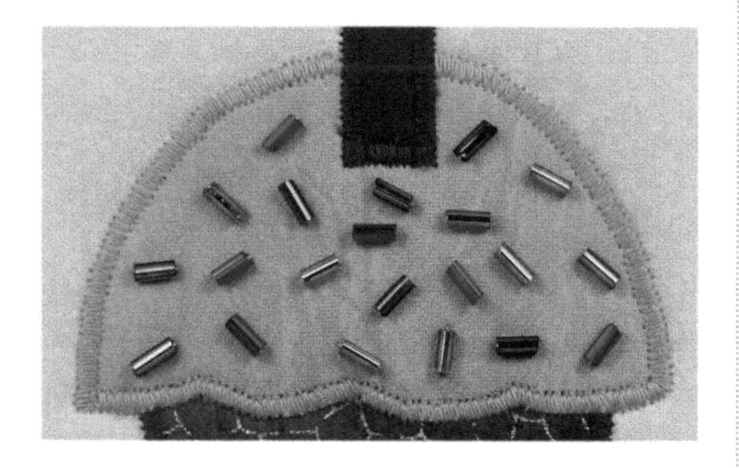

I have used small Bugle beads but seed beads work well as well. I find a beading needle is too fine to stitch through all the layers of the postcard.

8) Pin the stabilised white fabric rectangle on the back and stitch around again and again until happy with the edge finish.

9) Mark the wick of the candle on with a Pigma Micron pen.

'Big' birthday postcard. Create the basic cupcake but use numbers for the candles.

I either use a stencil or generate the numbers from the computer. You must remember, when drawing them on the fusible web, they need to be in mirror image so when the fabric is applied to the postcard it is the right way round. Embroider on the cocktail sticks using split stitch.

For the flower decorated one I just added small flowers and leaves, the centre of the flowers can be either French knots or seed beads.

If putting it through the post and using seed beads, remember to protect the front of the postcard with a piece of paper or card.

For the Christmas cupcake, add on icing and holly leaves with beads for the berries.

For valentines and wedding anniversaries then the cupcake is decorated with hearts, two are appliqued and the small ones embroidered on.

Template for Cupcake

Extra Templates for Cupcake

Flower

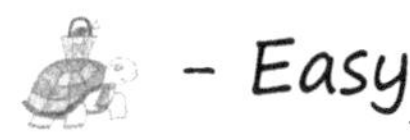 - Easy

The inspiration for this postcard was the paper cards I used to make before I found Quilted Postcards. I have designed it to look like layers of paper built up.

It makes a lovely Mother's Day or birthday postcard.

You will need to make this postcard

- 2 pieces of white cotton fabric 4½" x 6½"
- 2 pieces of iron-on interfacing 4½" x 6½"
- 1 piece of wadding 4" x 6"
- Fusible web
- A selection of fabrics
- A selection of sewing threads

The background for this Postcard is different from the Starter one in that it is pieced from two pieces of fabric.

1) For the background of the postcard cut the fabric for the bottom piece 2" x 6½" and the piece for the top 3" x 6½". Place one piece of the interfacing with the glue side up on the ironing area, place the two pieces of background fabric, right side up, on top just factionally overlapping and press onto the interfacing.

2) Draw the pattern pieces, 2½" Square, Flower and Flower Centre, onto the paper side of the fusible web and cut out with a ¼" extra all round.

3) Press onto the chosen fabrics and cut out on the line.

4) Press the design pieces onto the prepared background fabric.

5) Layer with the wadding and rectangle of white fabric.

6) Machine stitch the design, starting with the centre of the flower and working outwards.

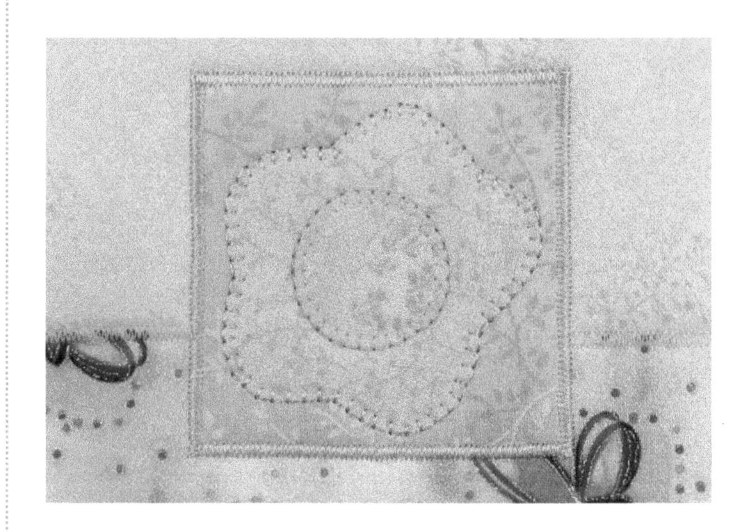

The reason why I do not overlap the two base fabrics too much is that it will cause a thickness in the card when stitched.

7) Pin the stabilised white fabric rectangle on the back and stitch around again and again until happy with the edge finish.

With this variation, I have used the flower head on its own, but embroidered a stem and added leaves and made it look like it is in a field of other flowers.

Use just the centres in a row with button centres and embroider on the stems, leaves and ground.

Old shirt buttons make great centres to flowers.

The whole background is covered with flowers, the centres can be plain, embroidered or quilted to change the look.

For a more stylised look, then just use the centres and embroider on stylised stems.

Template for Flower

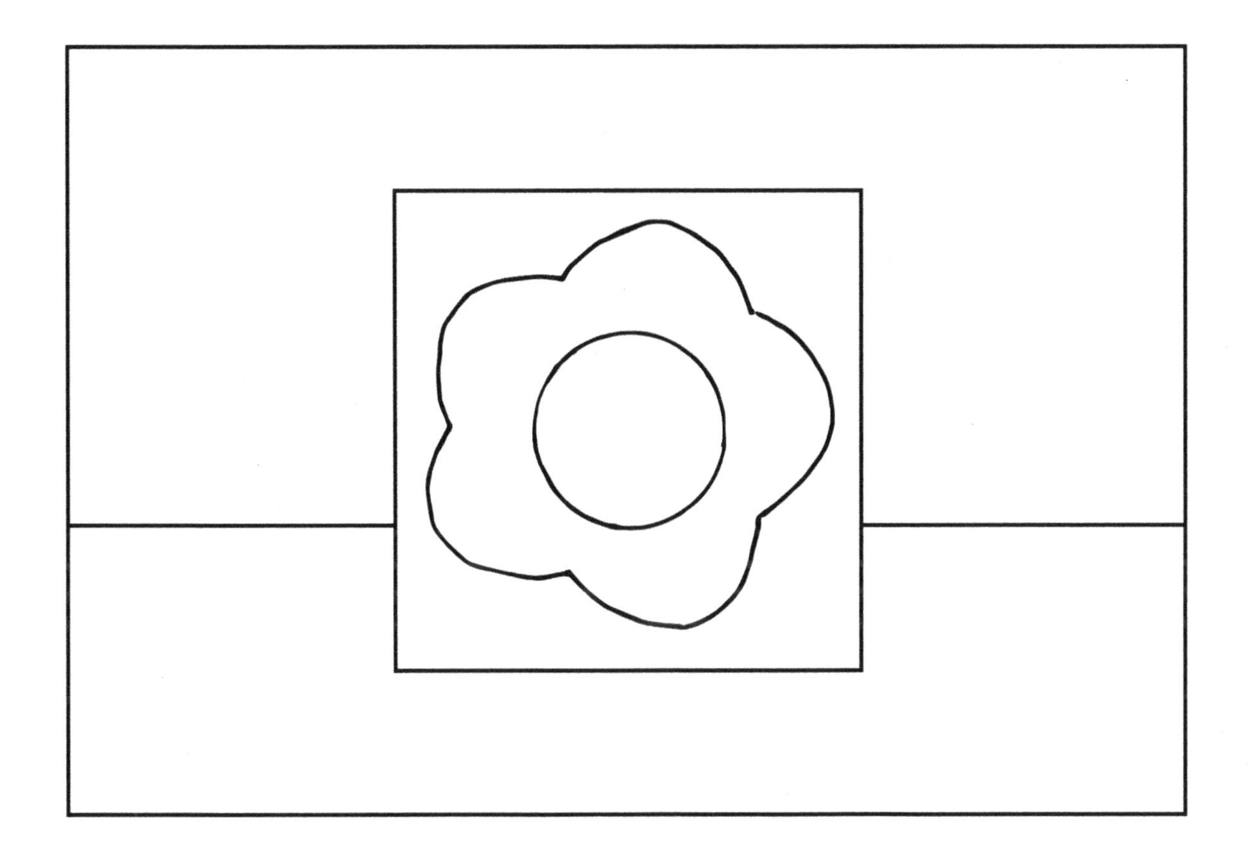

Extra Templates for Flower

Christmas Tree

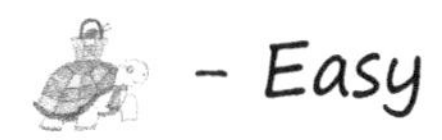 - Easy

Christmas is a time when I make a batch of Quilted Postcards for close family and a few special friends, I tend to make one design but vary it to make each postcard individual.

A theme that I use a lot, not only in Postcards but in all my creative work is the tree motif - so it has to be used at Christmas.

You will need to make this postcard

- 2 pieces of white cotton fabric 4½" x 6½"
- 2 pieces of iron-on interfacing 4½" x 6½"
- 1 piece of wadding 4" x 6"
- Fusible web
- A selection of fabrics
- A selection of sewing threads, including metallic gold thread
- Star sequin

1) Draw the pattern pieces, Tree and the Pot onto the paper side of the fusible web and cut out with a ¼" extra all round.

2) Press onto the chosen fabrics and cut out on the line.

3) Press the design pieces onto the prepared background fabric.

4) Layer with the wadding and rectangle of white fabric.

5) Machine stitch the design.

I have used zig-zag round the tree and pot but I have used straight stitch for the gold thread decoration. When using metallic thread please remember to use a Metallic or Top Stitch needle, it stops the frustration of constantly breaking thread.

6) Stitch on a Star sequin.

7) Pin the stabilised white fabric rectangle on the back and stitch around again and again until happy with the edge finish.

Sew strips of different green fabric together to make the tree, then decorate with small red seed beads.

Use three smaller trees to create the postcard, the decoration on the trees is more angular and I have used miniature buttons as decorations on the pots.

Change the shape of the tree and pot and use modern colours to completely change the look of the postcard.

Templates for Christmas Tree

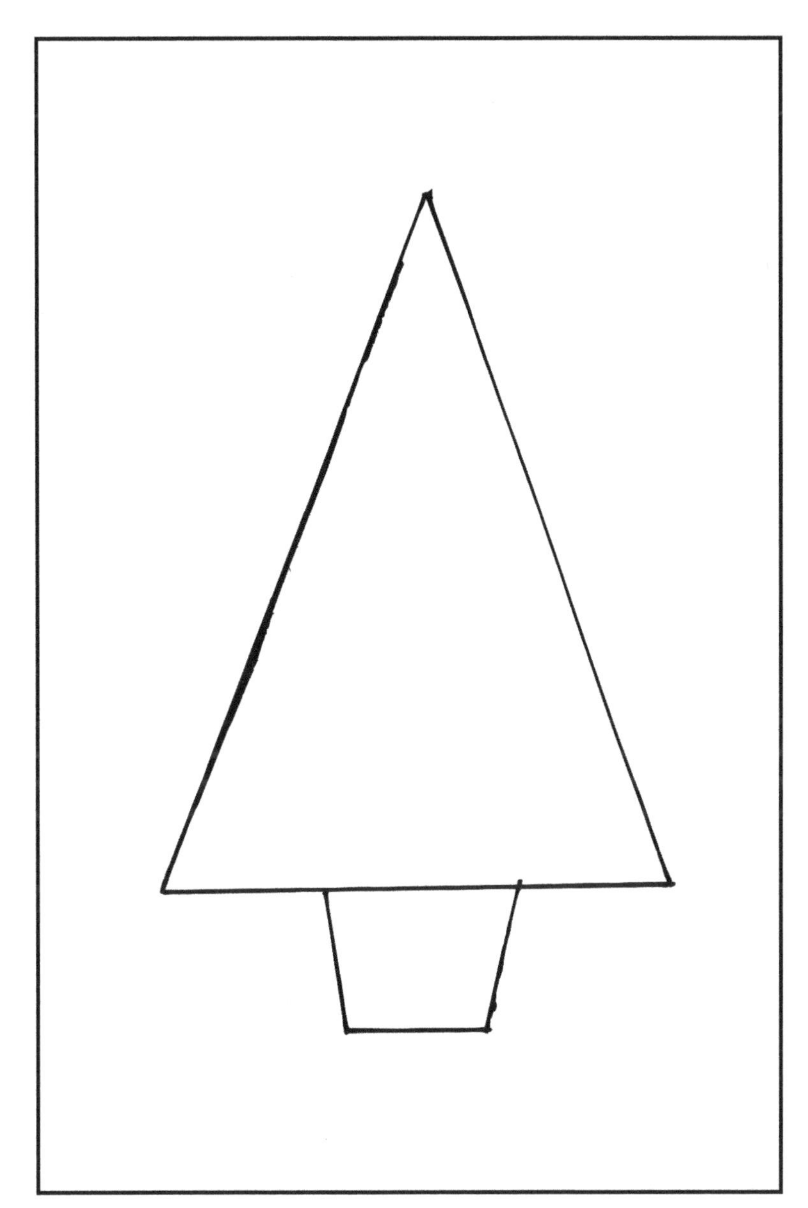

Extra Templates for Christmas Tree

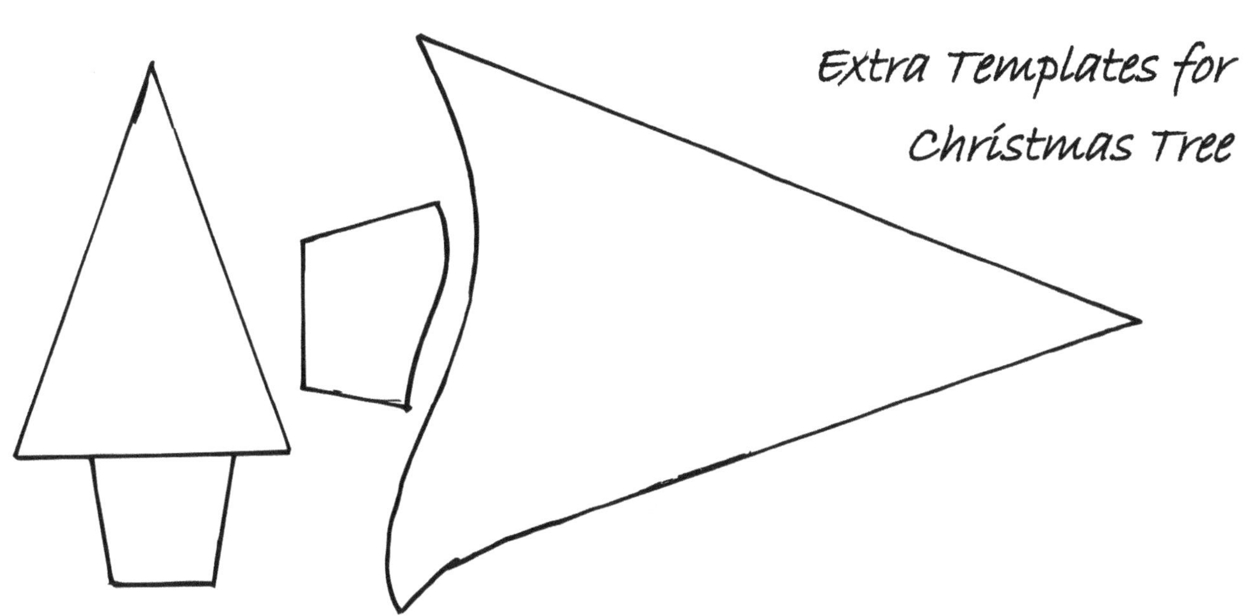

Shoe

 - Easy

The inspiration for this card is the classic black court shoe and from that you can create some wonderful decorative, fantasy shoes – Cinderella shoes.

I have a complete love/hate relationship with footwear. I love looking at the beautifully embroidered shoes and boots of the centuries past and the pretty sandals and wedding shoes available now, but I know that none of them will ever fit me as I have the most horrendously wide feet!!! I could just about fit the shoe boxes! Total shoe envy, so instead I just create shoes and boots on fabric Postcards.

You will need to make this postcard

- 2 pieces of white cotton fabric 4½" x 6½"
- 2 pieces of iron-on interfacing 4½" x 6½"
- 1 piece of wadding 4" x 6"
- Fusible web
- A selection of fabrics
- A selection of sewing threads

The background for this postcard is different from the Starter one in that it is made from two pieces of fabric hemmed together.

1) For the background take two pieces of fabric, one piece 2½" x 4½" and the second 4½" square. Pin right sides together, stitch with a ¼" seam.

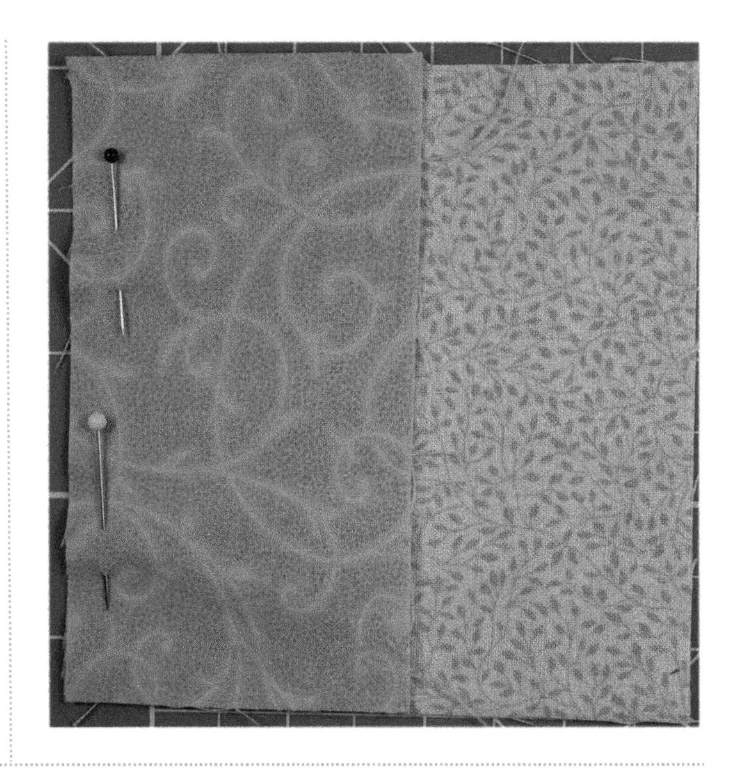

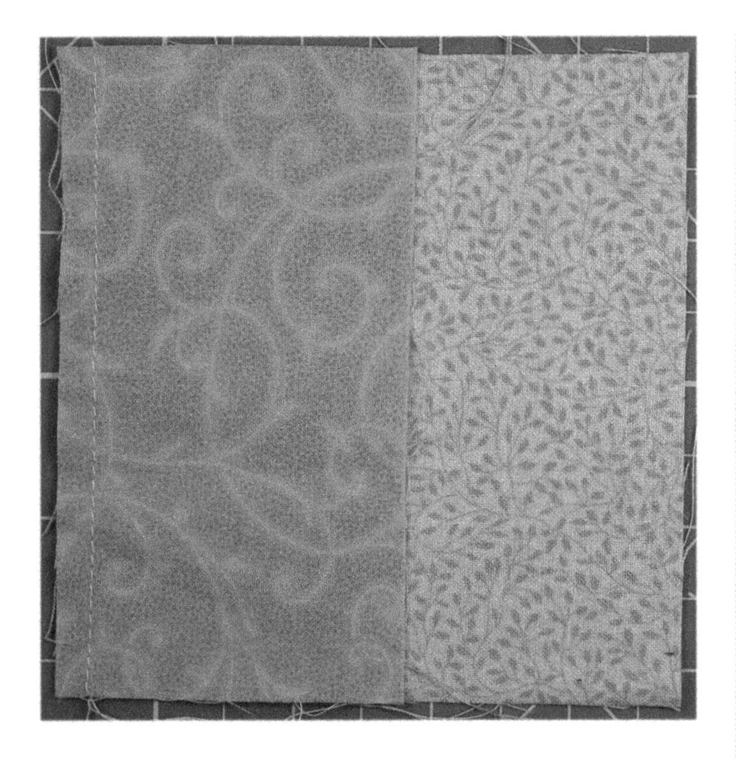

2) Press the seam open and then work as for a one-piece background.

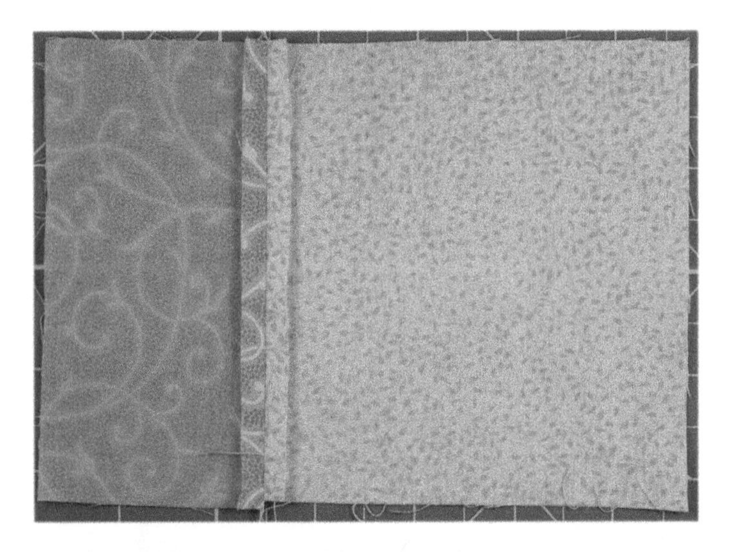

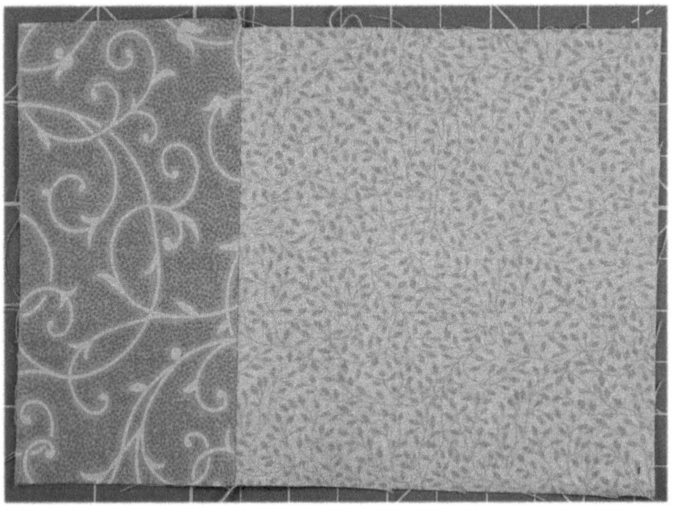

3) Draw the pattern piece for the shoe onto the paper side of the fusible web and cut out with a ¼" extra all round.

4) Press onto the chosen fabrics and cut out on the line.

5) Press the design pieces onto the prepared background fabric.

6) Draw on the details to be stitched - the line at the top of the heel.

7) Layer with the wadding and rectangle of white fabric.

8) Machine stitch the design - straight stitch a long top of heel.

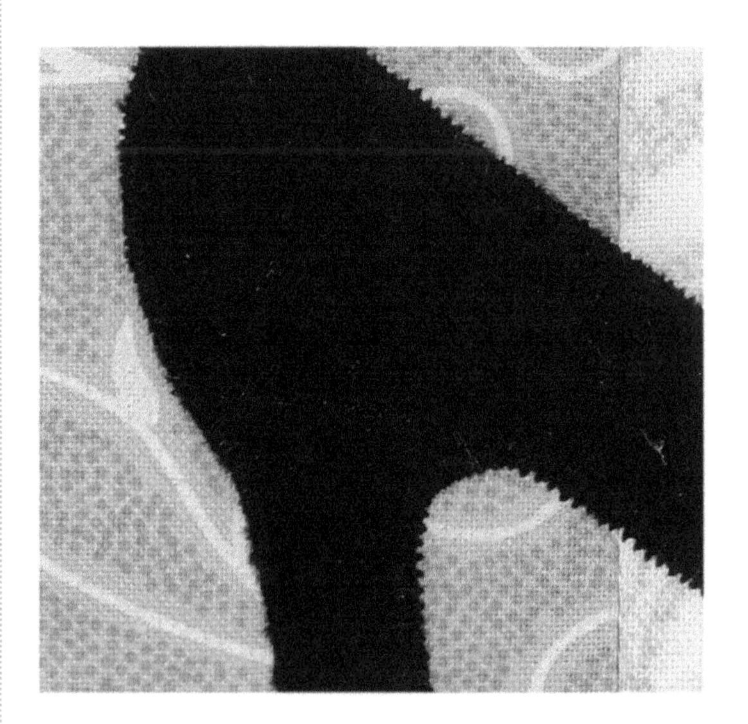

9) Pin the stabilised white fabric rectangle on the back and stitch around again and again until happy with the edge finish.

I have used the original pattern, but used two different floral fabrics, one for the heel and the other for the shoe, giving a soft, romantic look to the shoe.

With the red mule, I have removed the toe and back of the shoe and elongated the top and then added a ribbon decoration.

I have stitched the sole and heel in a different colour to add definition.

For the fantasy shoe, I have used a sparkly fabric, extended the front of the shoes up and removed the back and then decorated with beads and sequins.

I have made this in ivory silk as a wedding congratulations card.

Template for Shoe

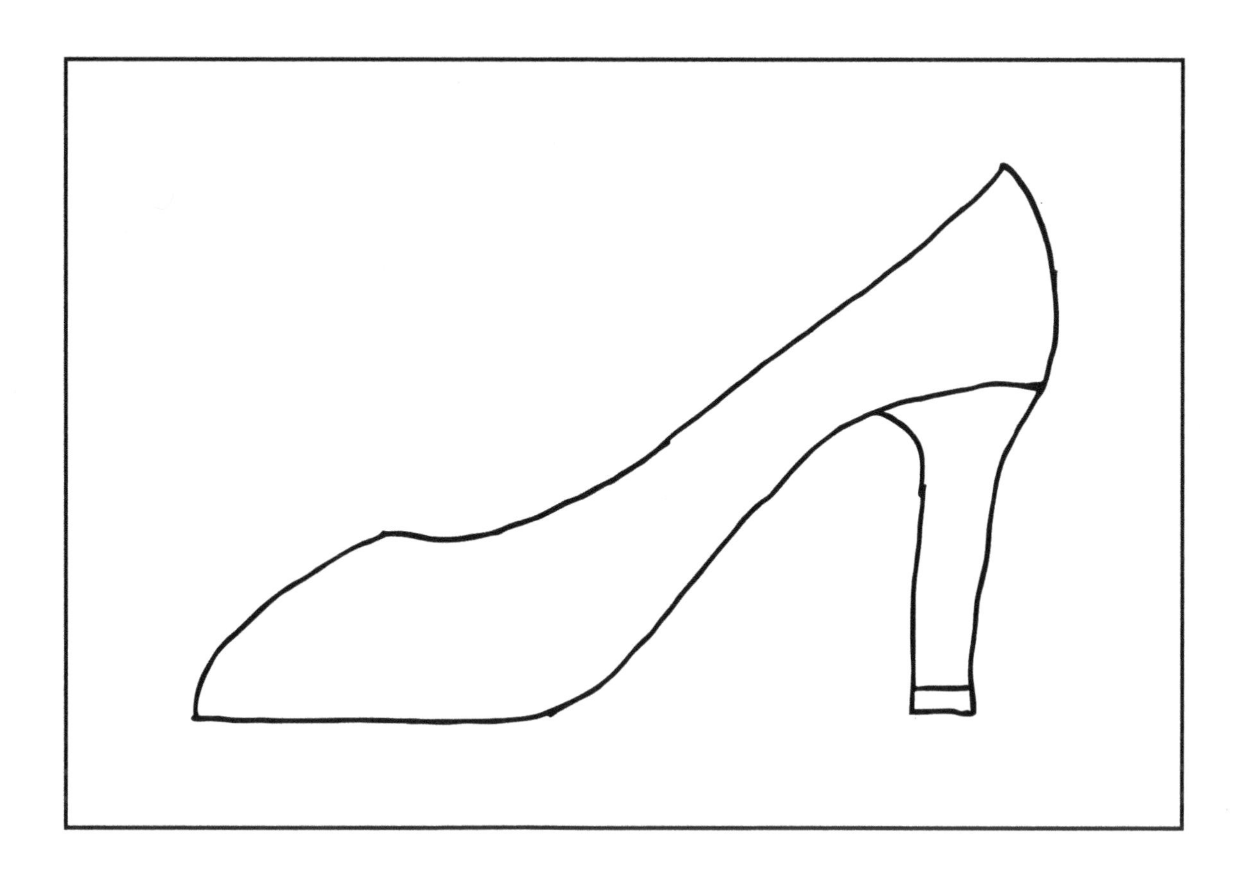

Extra Templates for Shoe

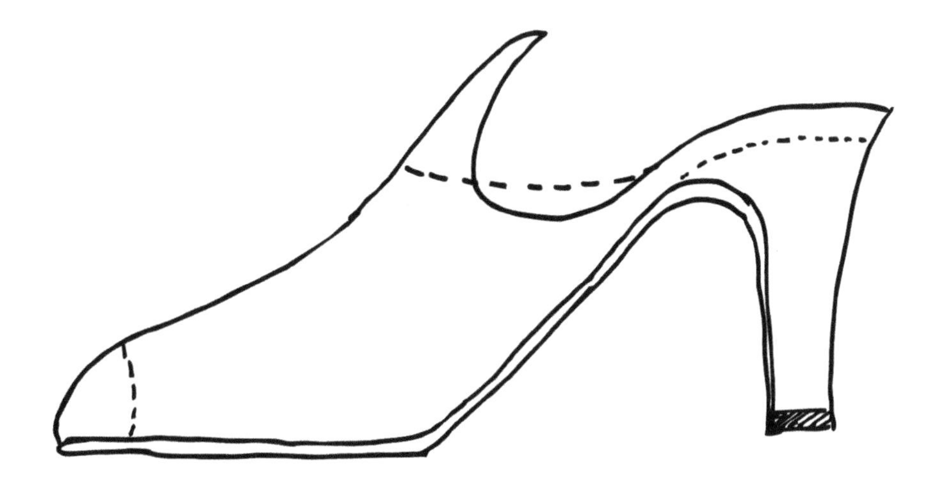

Dress

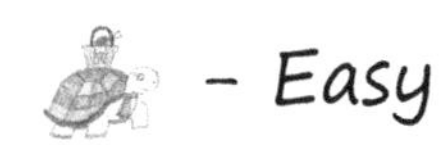 - Easy

This postcard takes its inspiration from the lovely tea dresses of the 1950's, with their simple shape and full skirts, very elegant.

I have always loved historical, theatre, film and fantasy inspired fashion but have never been brave enough to wear it, and so I am never short of ideas for postcards and wall art pieces.

You will need to make this postcard

- 2 pieces of white cotton fabric 4½" x 6½"
- 2 pieces of iron-on interfacing 4½" x 6½"
- 1 piece of wadding 4" x 6"
- Fusible web
- A selection of fabrics
- A selection of sewing threads
- A selection of stranded embroidery cottons
- Black Micron Pigma pen

1) Draw the pattern pieces for the Dress and the Dressmaker's Dummy, onto the paper side of the fusible web and cut out with a ¼" extra all round.

2) Press onto the chosen fabrics and cut out on the line.

3) Press the design pieces onto the prepared background fabric.

4) Draw on the details of the belt and lines up the skirt to create the folds. These will be stitched later.

5) Layer with the wadding and rectangle of white fabric.

6) Machine stitch the design.

For the dressmaker's dummy I have used straight stitch.

7) Hand embroider on the flower choker necklace.

8) Draw on the pole of the Dressmaker's Dummy at the bottom with the Pigma pen.

9) Pin the stabilised white fabric rectangle on the back and stitch around again and again until happy with the edge finish.

With the blue version I have changed the neckline and added a wide belt.

The basic dress is the same, just created in a floral fabric, but I have added a wider belt.

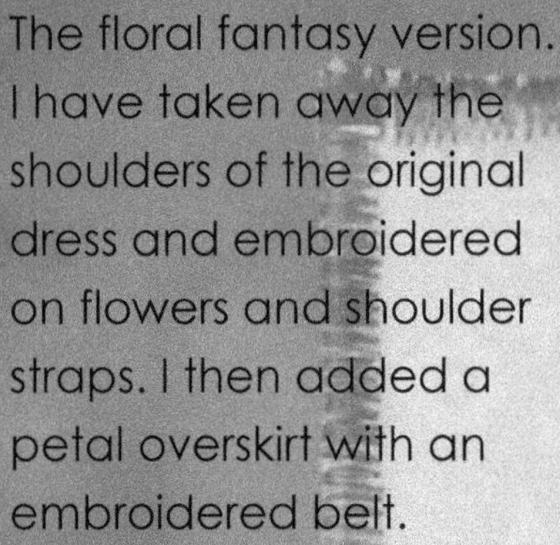

The floral fantasy version. I have taken away the shoulders of the original dress and embroidered on flowers and shoulder straps. I then added a petal overskirt with an embroidered belt.

There are so many versions of this variation, maybe a Christmas version with holly leaves in red and green?

Template for Dress

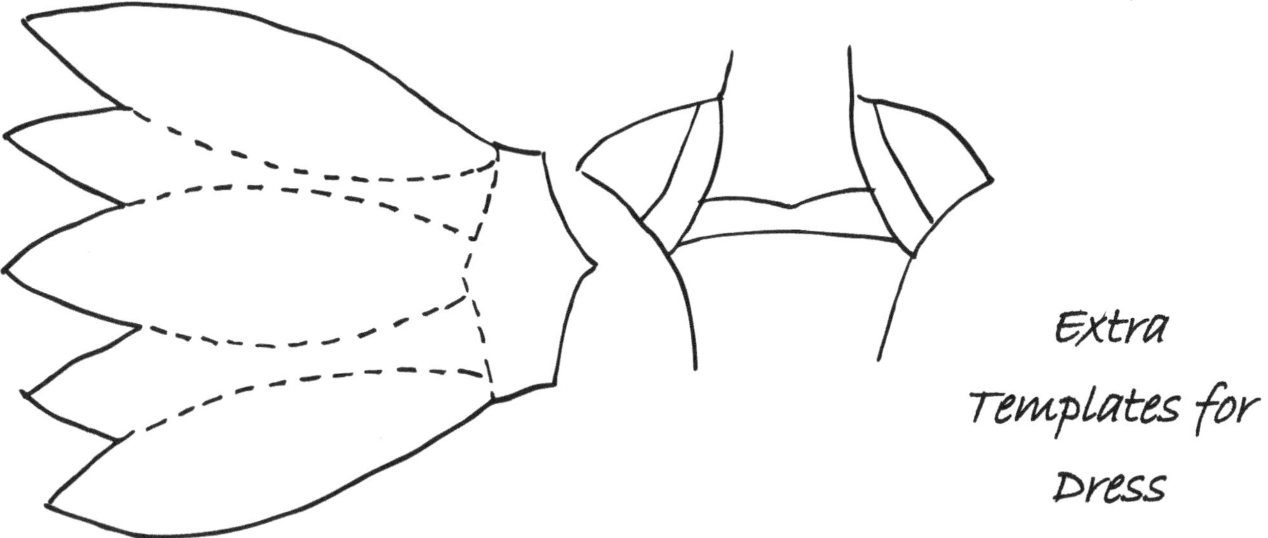

Extra Templates for Dress

Butterfly

- Intermediate

The inspiration for this postcard was a display of Victorian butterflies. The Victorians had a love of creating collections of butterflies and moths and stuffed animals, all rather odd but in a weird way beautiful! Most Stately homes seem to have a collection.

You will need to make this postcard

- 2 pieces of white cotton fabric 4½" x 6½"
- 2 pieces of iron-on interfacing 4½" x 6½"
- 1 piece of wadding 4" x 6"
- Fusible web
- A selection of fabrics
- A selection of sewing threads
- Stranded embroidery cotton
- A selection of beads and sequins

1) Draw the pattern pieces, Upper and Lower Wings, Wing Decoration and Body, onto the paper side of the fusible web and cut out with a ¼" extra all round.

2) Press onto the chosen fabrics and cut out on the line.

3) Press the design pieces onto the prepared background fabric.

4) Layer with the wadding and rectangle of white fabric.

5) Machine stitch the design.

6) Draw on the antenna and then embroider them.

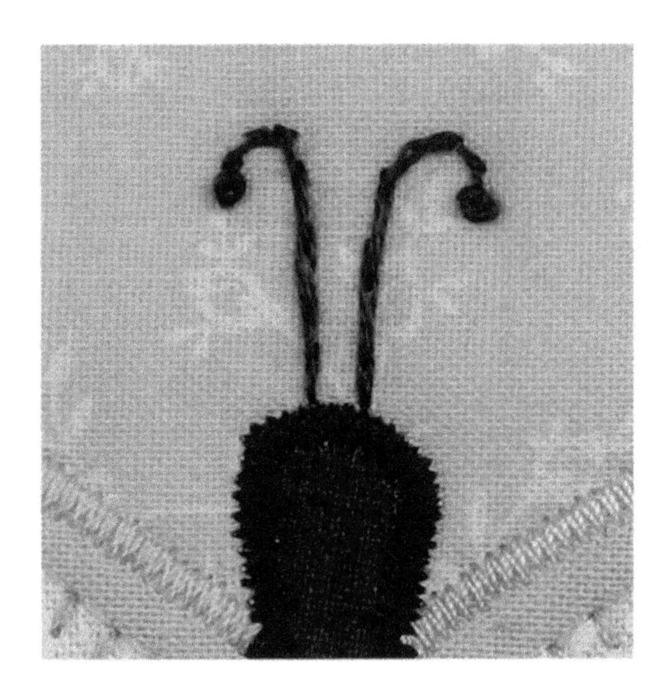

7) Stitch the beads and sequins in place.

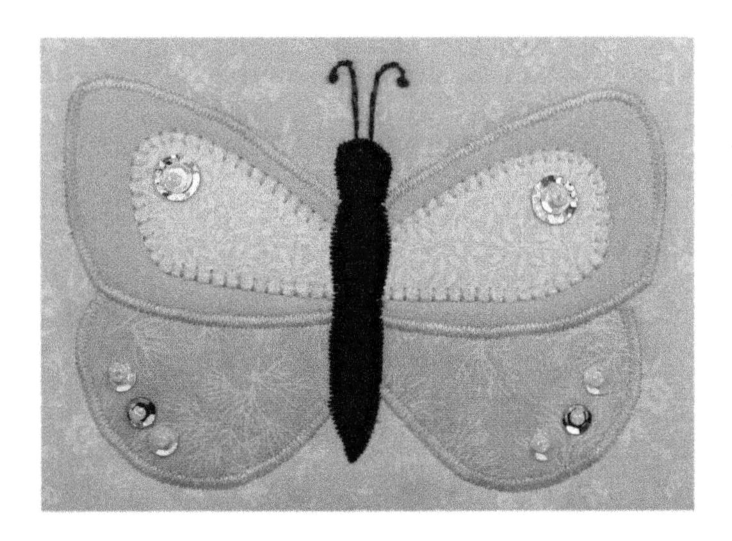

The amount of beads and sequins you use is personal preference, I don't use many as that's how I like it. If you don't want to use beads and sequins then you can embroider the details.

8) Pin the stabilised white fabric rectangle on the back and stitch around again and again until happy with the edge finish.

I have found that when I am using variegated thread round the edge of a postcard to finish it, that it is best to do the first times round in a base plain colour and then only use the variegated thread for the final round of stitching. It gives better colour definition.

The blue variation is the same as the original but in blue!

This one is small butterflies and flowers. With additional stems embroidered onto the design.

For the flower and butterfly, I have used just the body and one set of wings to make it look like the butterfly is flying to the flower in the corner.

Template for Butterfly

Extra Templates for Butterfly

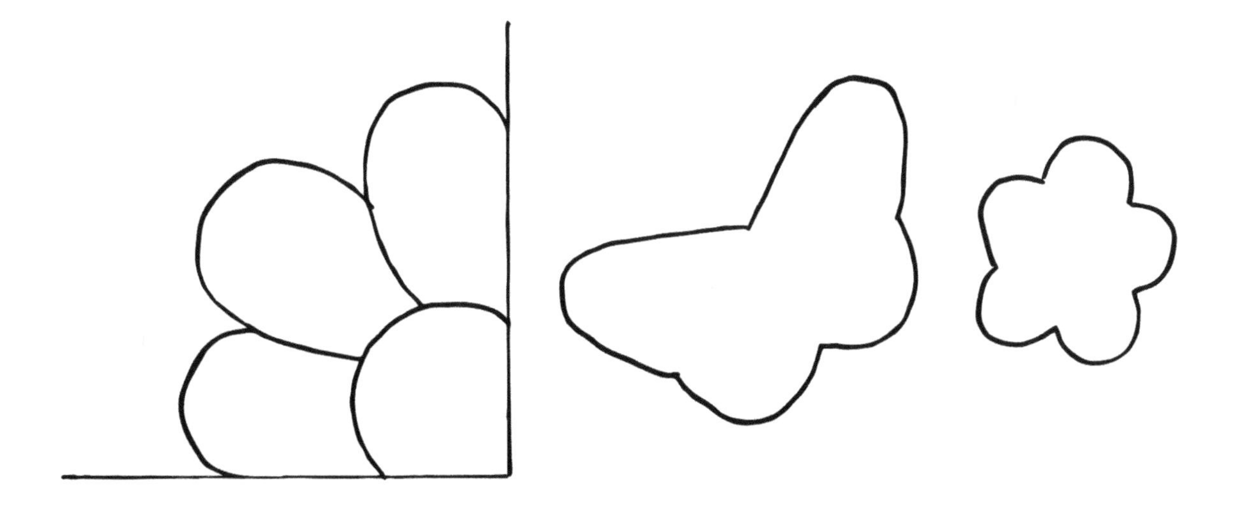

Letter

- Intermediate

Letters are a great gift for anyone – from a baby gift or christening and then just a birthday or wedding. They work for all ages and both men and women. They can be simple or complicated. You can even make a whole set to make up a name.

There is a lot of different things you can add to your Letter - embroider, applique, words or charms - to make each one individual.

You will need to make this postcard

- 3 pieces of white cotton fabric 4½" x 6½"
- 2 pieces of iron-on interfacing 4½" x 6½"
- 1 piece of wadding 4" x 6"
- Fusible web
- A selection of fabrics
- A selection of sewing threads
- A selection of stranded embroidery cottons
- Black Micron Pigma pen

The background for this postcard is worked in yet a different way from those already shown in the book, all my landscape ones are worked using this method.

1) Draw the Background Landscape pieces onto the paper side of the fusible web and cut out with a ¼" extra all round.

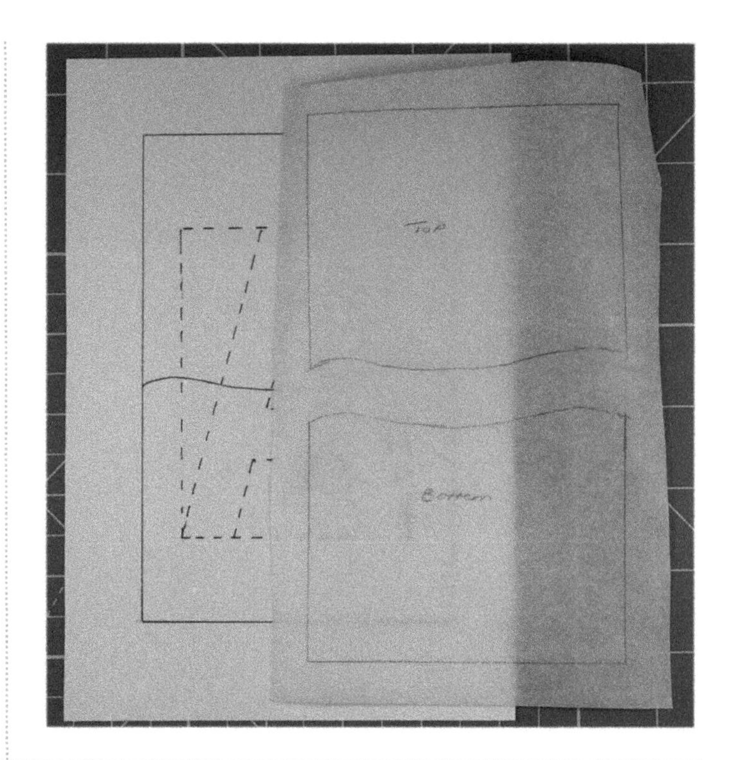

2) Press onto the chosen fabrics and just cut along the joining line, i.e. the bottom of the sky section (Top) and the top of the meadow/grass section (Bottom).

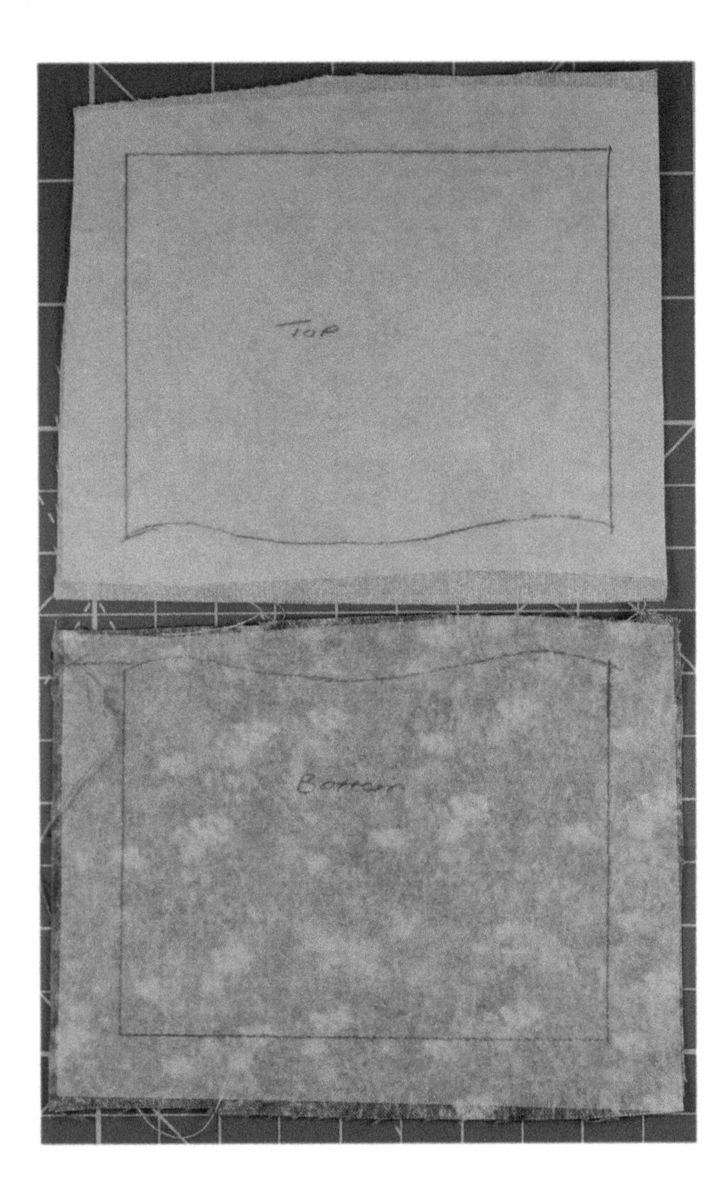

I don't cut out round the edges, as this would be 4" x 6" finished size and I find that by keeping the fabric background bigger and then trimming down at the end I get a better finish to the postcard.

3) Press the design pieces onto a piece of the white fabric.

4) Mark the 4" x 6" rectangle on the front of the fabric.

Make sure the 4" x 6" square is central so that it covers all of the backing fabric.

5) Press one piece of iron-on interfacing onto the back of the design.

The rest of the postcard makeup is now the same as it is for the other designs.

6) Draw the Letter onto the paper side of the fusible web, remember that it needs to be mirror image, and cut out with a ¼" extra all round.

7) Press onto the chosen fabrics and cut out on the line.

8) Position on the background, centrally, and press.

9) Layer with the wadding and rectangle of white fabric.

10) Machine stitch the design.

I have added lines of straight stitching onto the grass to create contours.

11) Embroider on the grass.

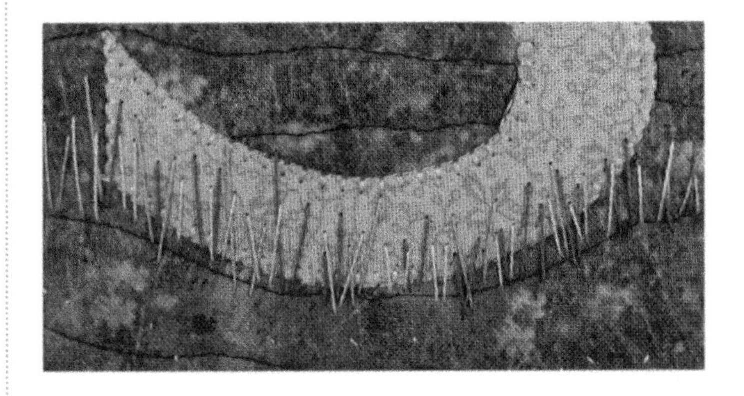

12) Draw on the "birds".

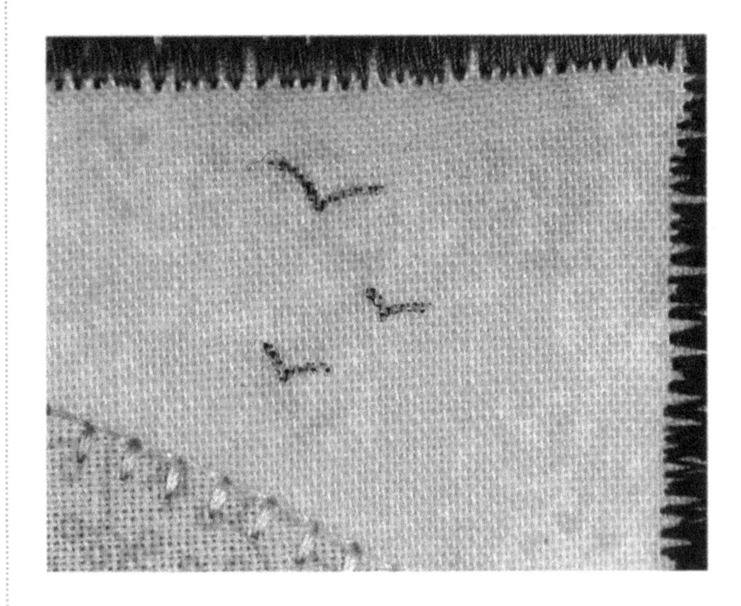

13) Pin the stabilised white fabric rectangle on the back and stitch around again and again until happy with the edge finish.

This is a far more complicated version of the basic Letter, with the letter embroidered with a climbing flowering plant.

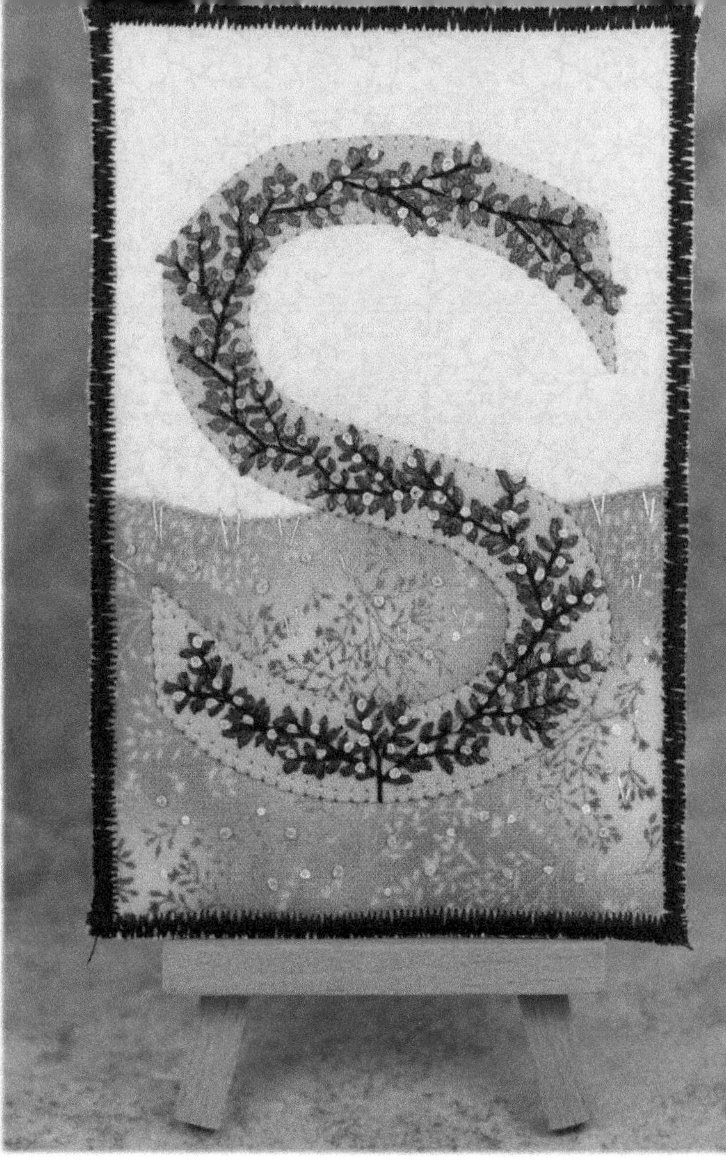

With the embroidered French Knot flowers I used a variegated stranded cotton, one thread colour but from light to dark shade.

This is a beach version, with sand, sea and sky, so the background is created from three pieces of fabric and more contour lines have been stitched and it has a kite as decoration.

The third version has a one piece background that is machine embroidered/quilted first, and then the letter appliqued on afterwards.

I layered and quilted the decoration, using some of the decorative embroidery stitches on my sewing machine and then zig-zag between the stitched areas. The letter is more ornamental and is pressed in place after background has been stitched.

Template for Letter

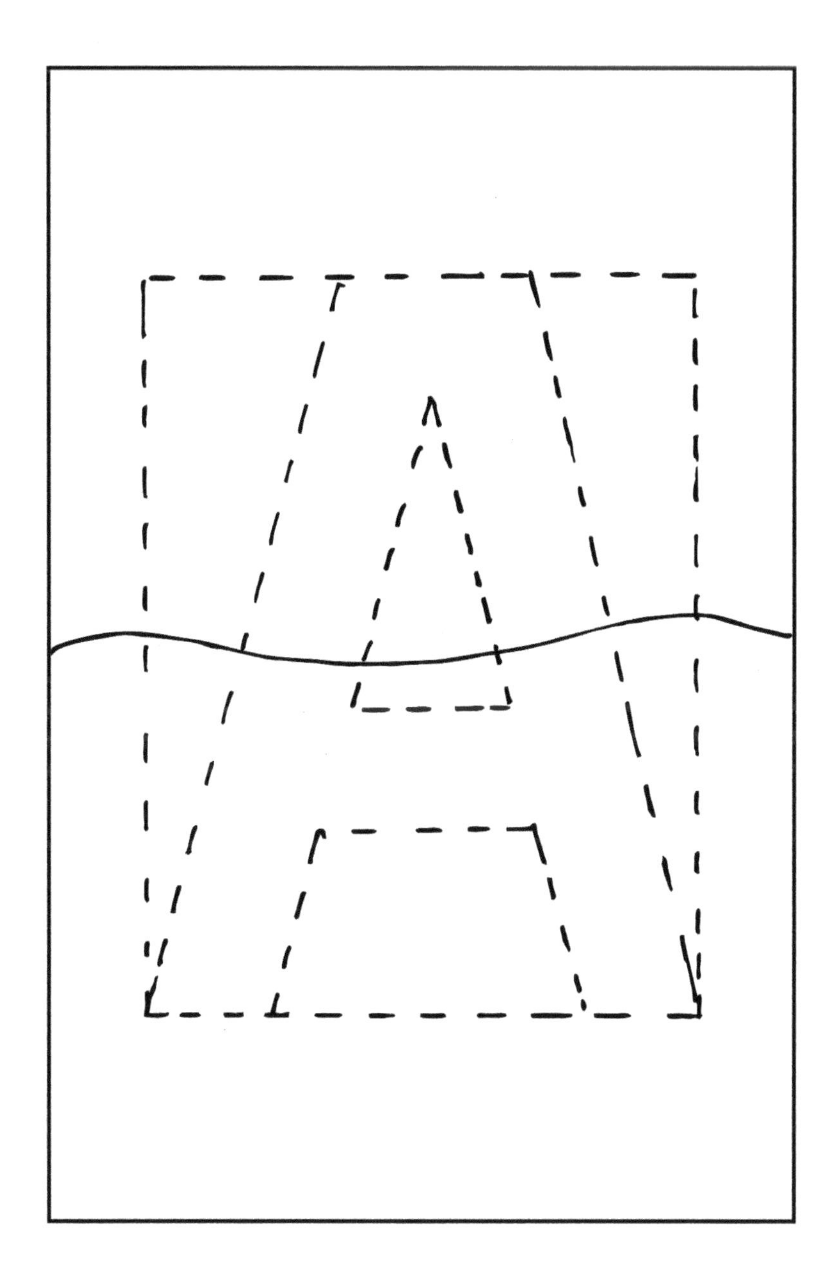

The hardest thing with Letters is getting the size and shape right, you can print them off or use a stencil. On the template pattern, I have created a dotted outline for the best size for a letter and also marked on an 'A' so you have an idea of the size. I used an 'A' as it's the first letter of the alphabet and it doesn't have a right or wrong way!

New Home

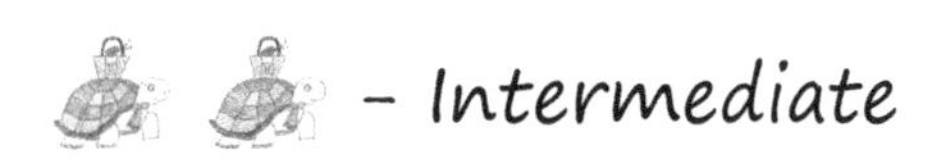

- Intermediate

It's nice to send a card when someone moves home, the basic postcard looks very simple, but because of the smallness of the pieces being stitched it is fiddlier than it looks. By adding bits, you can change the look very easily.

You will need to make this postcard

- 2 pieces of white cotton fabric 4½" x 6½"
- 2 pieces of iron-on interfacing 4½" x 6½"
- 1 piece of wadding 4" x 6"
- Fusible web
- A selection of fabrics
- A selection of sewing threads

1) Draw the House, Door, Window and Roof onto the paper side of the fusible web and cut out with a ¼" extra all round.

2) Press onto the chosen fabrics and cut out on the line.

3) Press the design pieces onto the prepared background fabric.

4) Layer with the wadding and rectangle of white fabric.

With a design this size I make the stitch length shorter than the standard length. It makes it easier to stitch in smaller pieces. The front door has lines of stitching up and down it to give depth. It may look like I have used a black thread but I have actually used a very dark grey, this isn't as 'hard' as a black.

5) Machine stitch the design.

6) Pin the stabilised white fabric rectangle on the back and stitch around a number of times.

I have added lots more details, I have drawn on the roof tiles and blocks on the walls using a Pigma pen. Then I have embroidered plants in a window box and along the bottom of the house. I have also added a tree and shrubs round the house.

Template for New Home

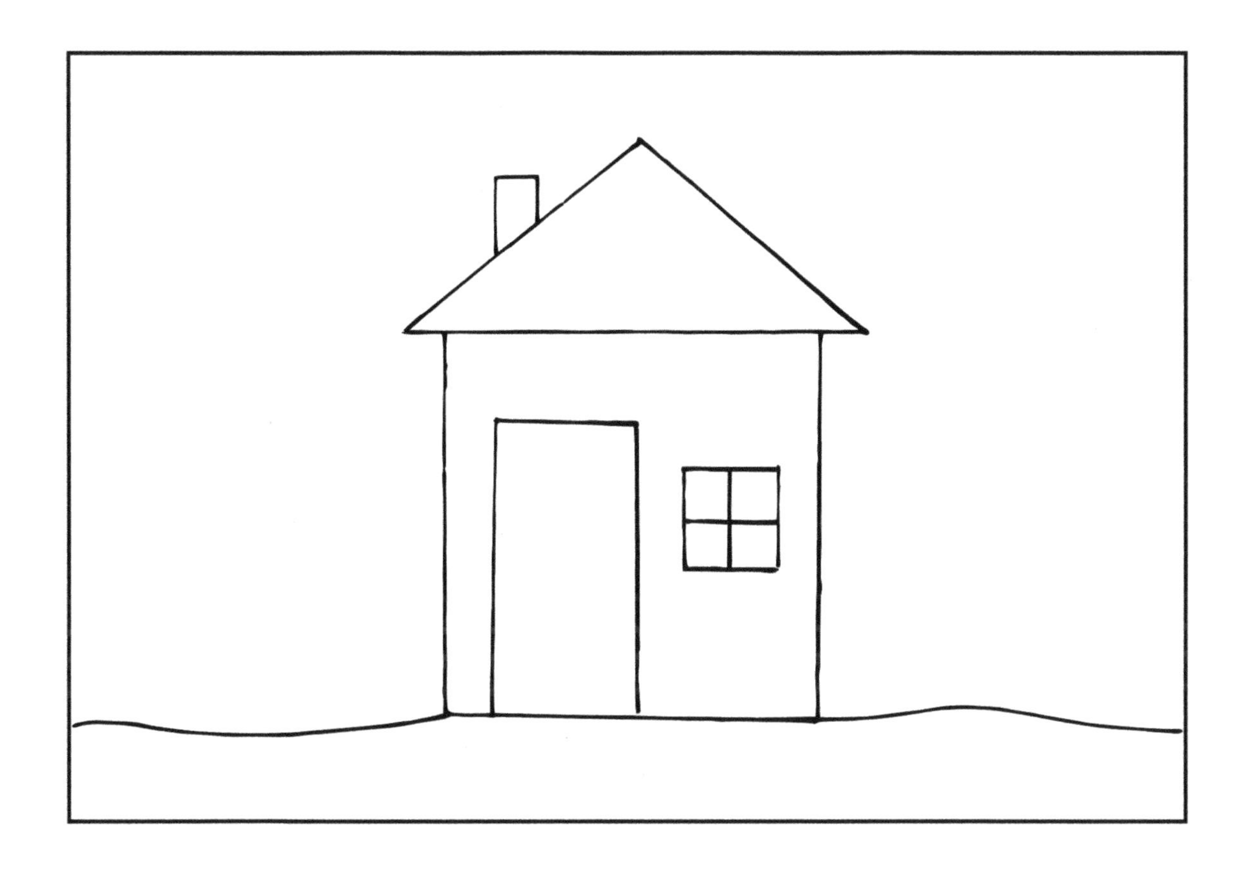

Extra Templates for New Home

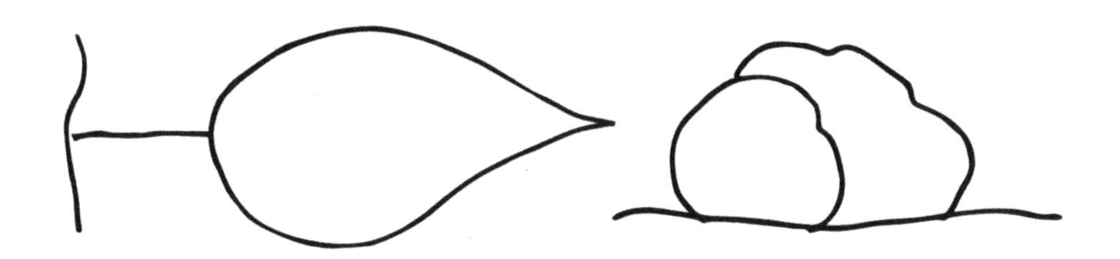

Shirt

- Intermediate

Before I made Quilted Postcards for my husband, I made him very individual ties and so, this postcard came out of the idea of ties. It is a good postcard for any man's birthday but also Father's Day.

You will need to make this postcard

- 2 pieces of white cotton fabric 4½" x 6½"
- 2 pieces of iron-on interfacing 4½" x 6½"
- 1 piece of wadding 4" x 6"
- Fusible web
- A selection of fabrics
- A selection of sewing threads

1) Draw the Shirt and Tie onto the paper side of the fusible web and cut out with a ¼" extra all round.

2) Press onto the chosen fabrics and cut out on the line.

3) Press the design pieces onto the prepared background and draw on the details to be stitched.

4) Layer with the wadding and rectangle of white fabric.

5) Machine stitch the design.

6) Pin the stabilised white fabric rectangle on the back and stitch around a number of times.

The same design is used for the variation but in a different colourway.

The second version is without the tie, I then stitched in the button band and have made the shirt in a floral fabric. You could also change the colour of the collar, button band and pocket for another variation.

Template for Shirt

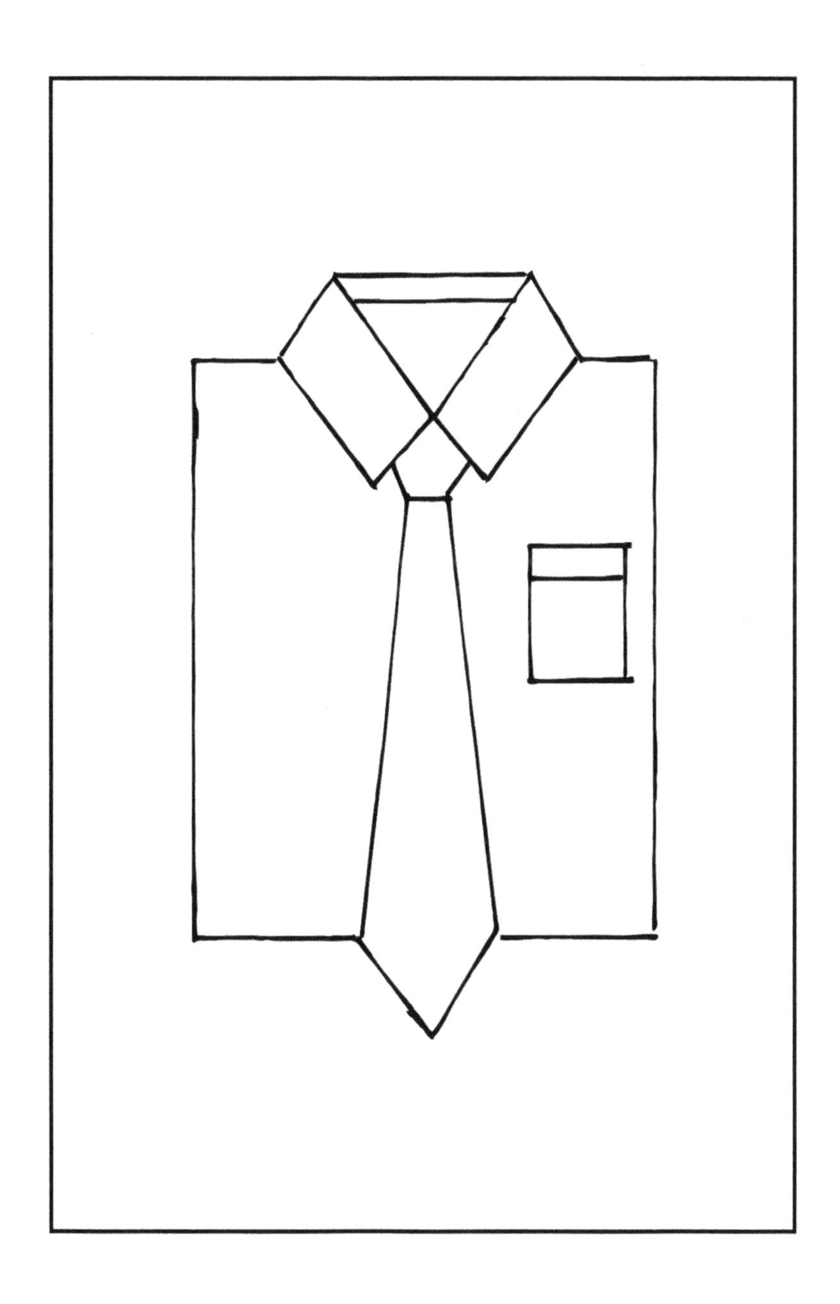

Easter

- Intermediate

The original inspiration for the eggs was an Easter activity pack our daughter had as a child! It included eggs to colour and make up into an Easter Card.

The eggs can look totally different just by the fabrics used and the thread, I have gone for a simpler look with mine, but you can be as wild as you like.

You will need to make this postcard

- 2 pieces of white cotton fabric 4½" x 6½"
- 2 pieces of iron-on interfacing 4½" x 6½"
- 1 piece of wadding 4" x 6"
- Fusible web
- A selection of fabrics
- A selection of sewing threads
- A selection of stranded embroidery cottons

1) Draw the 3" Square, The Strip and the 2 Eggs onto the paper side of the fusible web and cut out with a ¼" extra all round.

2) Press onto the chosen fabrics and cut out on the line.

With pieces like the decorative strip on this postcard I would recommend that you don't run it all the way across the postcard, even though it seems easier to get it level, only have it where it shows. Having it run right across the postcards, adds another layer to sew through and it can create a 'shadow' on the top square.

3) Press the design pieces onto the prepared background.

4) Layer with the wadding and rectangle of white fabric.

5) Mark the decoration on the eggs and then machine stitch the design.

6) Embroider on the grass and use French knots to create flowers.

7) Pin the stabilised white fabric rectangle on the back and stitch around a number of times.

Instead of the small eggs, you can use one large egg, which can be decorated in lots of ways.

This variation has four eggs and an Easter bunny, I have created her in brown but she works just as well in white.

Flowers and a single large egg are another way of decorating this postcard.

I have used five of the eggs in different colours with slightly different stitched details on them. Then I have added more grass and flower details.

Template for Easter

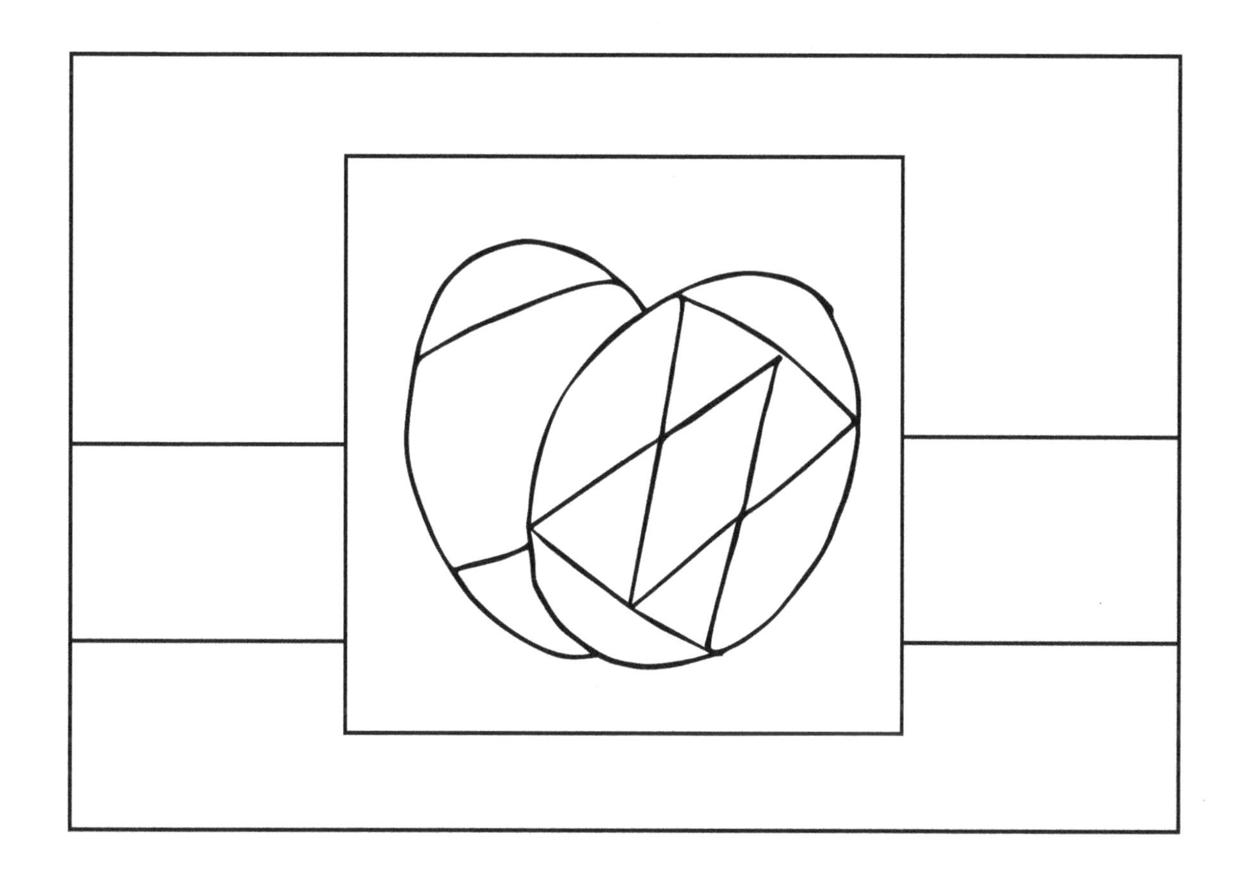

Extra Templates for Easter

Christmas Holly

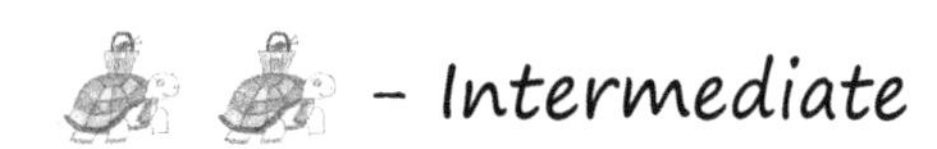
- Intermediate

The inspiration for the holly and candle postcard came from a Christmas candle display my sister had one year, hers had three candles in deep red. It made a great photo and inspired me.

Christmas Holly can be used in so many ways.

You will need to make this postcard

- 2 pieces of white cotton fabric 4½" x 6½"
- 2 pieces of iron-on interfacing 4½" x 6½"
- 1 piece of wadding 4" x 6"
- Fusible web
- A selection of fabrics
- A selection of sewing threads
- Sequins
- Black Micron Pigma pen

1) Draw the Candle, Flame and the Holly onto the paper side of the fusible web and cut out with a ¼" extra all round.

2) Press onto the chosen fabrics and cut out on the line.

3) Press the design pieces onto the prepared background fabric.

4) Layer with the wadding and rectangle of white fabric.

5) Machine stitch the design.

I have used zig-zag on the edges of the holly to give more defined edge, but straight stitch up the centre of the leaves.

6) Stitch on the 'berries' and draw on the wick of the candle with the Pigma pen.

I have used blanket stitch round the candle and straight stitch on the flame.

7) Pin the stabilised white fabric rectangle on the back and stitch around a number of times.

I like beads but buttons or sequins are better if the postcard is going to be posted.

Use the holly leaves on their own to create a postcard.

You can paint them with silver fabric paint to give a frosted look. And remember you don't have to create them just in dark green fabric.

Use smaller holly to decorate a Christmas pudding, made using a 2½" circle.

Using a 2½" circle of fabric but this time as a bauble with the holly decorating the top.

Template for Christmas Holly

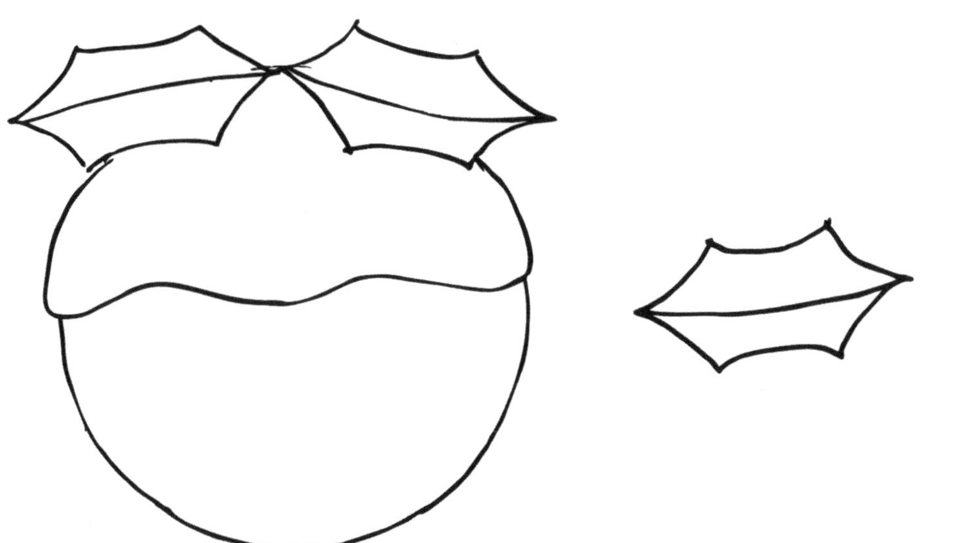

Extra Templates for Christmas Holly

New Baby

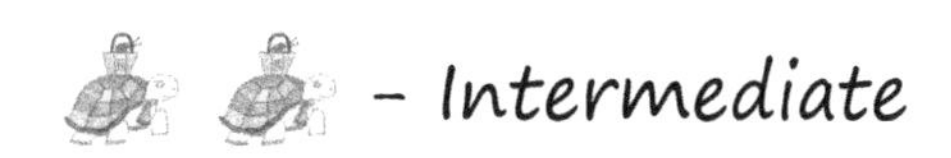

When a new baby comes into a family it is always a special time. A quilted postcard is a lovely keepsake. It can be mounted on a card or, if a ribbon is attached with buttons, it can hang on a door handle.

You will need to make this postcard

- 2 pieces of white cotton fabric 4½" x 6½"
- 2 pieces of iron-on interfacing 4½" x 6½"
- 1 piece of wadding 4" x 6"
- Fusible web
- A selection of fabrics
- A selection of sewing threads
- Miniature heart buttons

1) Draw the Pram and 3" x 4" Rectangle onto the paper side of the fusible web and cut out with a ¼" extra all round.

2) Press onto the chosen fabrics and cut out on the line.

3) Press the design pieces onto the prepared background fabric.

4) Draw on the handle and wheels with an air erasable pen.

I find that the end of a cotton reel is idea to draw round to create the wheels.

5) Layer with the wadding and rectangle of white fabric.

6) Machine stitch the design.

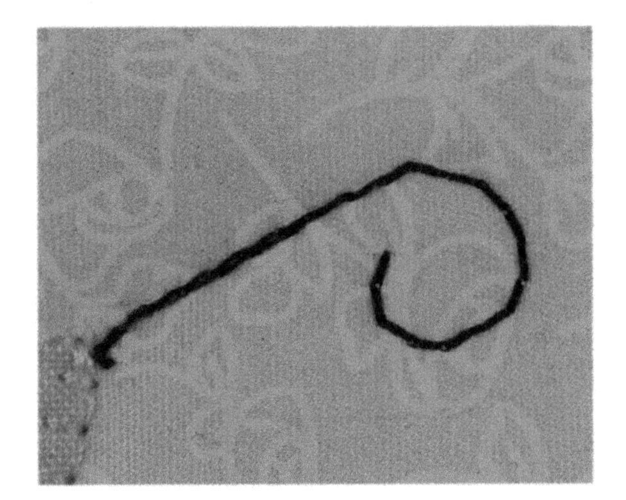

To stitch the handle and wheels use a smaller than standard stitch and take it very slowly. If you feel that it's too difficult to machine stitch them, then you can hand embroider the handle and wheels.

7) Stitch the miniature heart buttons onto the centre of the wheels.

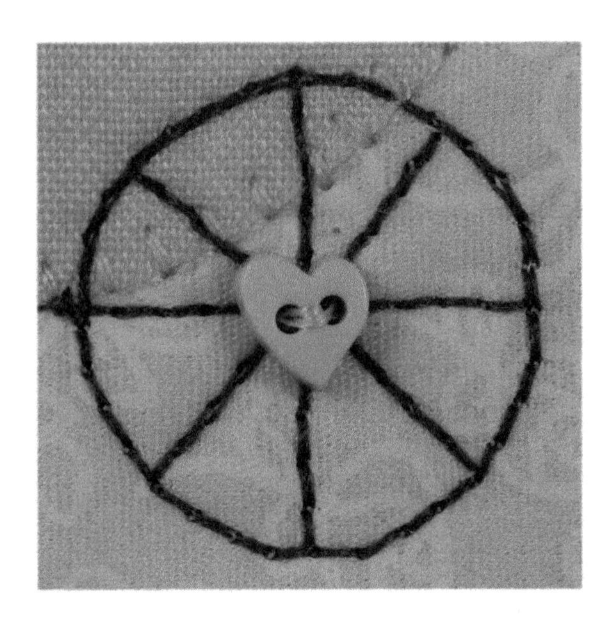

8) Pin the stabilised white fabric rectangle on the back and stitch around a number of times.

For twins, take away the rectangle background and use two prams facing each other and the handles create a heart in the middle of the design.

Template for New Baby

Landscape

- Expert

I have always loved landscapes and the countryside. I need my regular 'fix' of the countryside and our 'green' land, even if it's a few hours away from suburbia. We take lots of photos when we are out and so the landscape postcard is based on lots of different photos but gives a feel of England.

You will need to make this postcard

- 3 pieces of white cotton fabric 4½" x 6½"
- 2 pieces of iron-on interfacing 4½" x 6½"
- 1 piece of wadding 4" x 6"
- Fusible web
- A selection of fabrics
- A selection of sewing threads
- A selection of stranded embroidery cottons

The background to the landscape isn't very complicated to put together. It is created in the same way as the background for the Letter but with more layers/pieces. It is the details of the embroidery that make this a more complicated design.

1) Draw the pieces of the Landscape onto the paper side of the fusible web and cut out with a ¼" extra all round.

Remember to number the pieces this just makes it easier to put together.

2) Press onto the chosen fabrics and cut out on the line.

When cutting out the pieces for the landscape, I find that it gives a better finish if you only cut on the line where the pieces will meet each other and not the other edges.

3) Press the design pieces onto one of the pieces of the white fabric and draw on the 4" x 6" rectangle.

4) Press one piece of iron-on interfacing onto the back of the design.

5) Layer with the wadding and rectangle of white fabric.

6) Machine stitch the design.

7) Embroider on the flowers and grass.

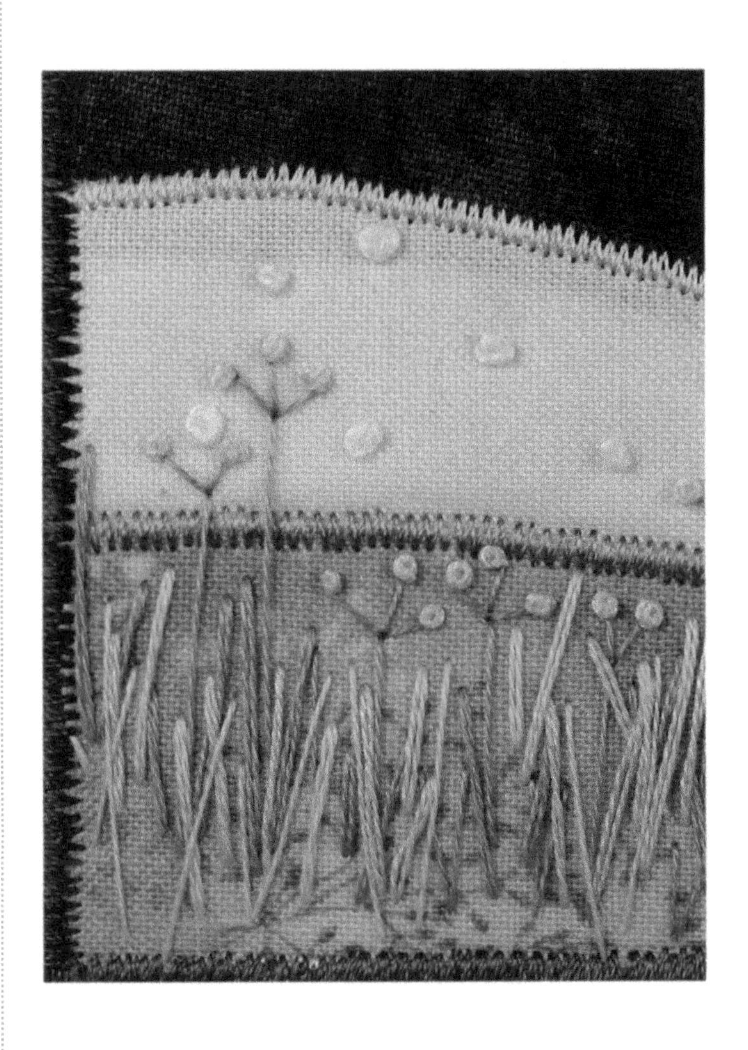

I have used French Knots for the flowers and long stitches to represent the grass.

8) Pin the stabilised white fabric rectangle on the back and stitch around a number of times.

Embroider bushes on the far hills, contour lines on the middle ones and tall grasses towards the front.

Using variegated green threads and lots of different shades of single stranded embroidery cotton from greens to browns adds depth to the grasses.

The sky is created using a patterned blue fabric and then just contour lines stitched onto the far hills. Bushes are stitched along the line of the middle hill to create a hedge line and then cow parsley has been stitched at the front.

I have changed the line of the hills slightly and taken away the front one. The far hills have contour lines and bushes embroidered on them. A fence line has been added across the edge of the middle hills and then the plants are stitched along the front.

I have removed the front hill, bought the fence line forward, and not stitched as many grasses at the front, but created a wild flower meadow with French knots.

Template for Landscape

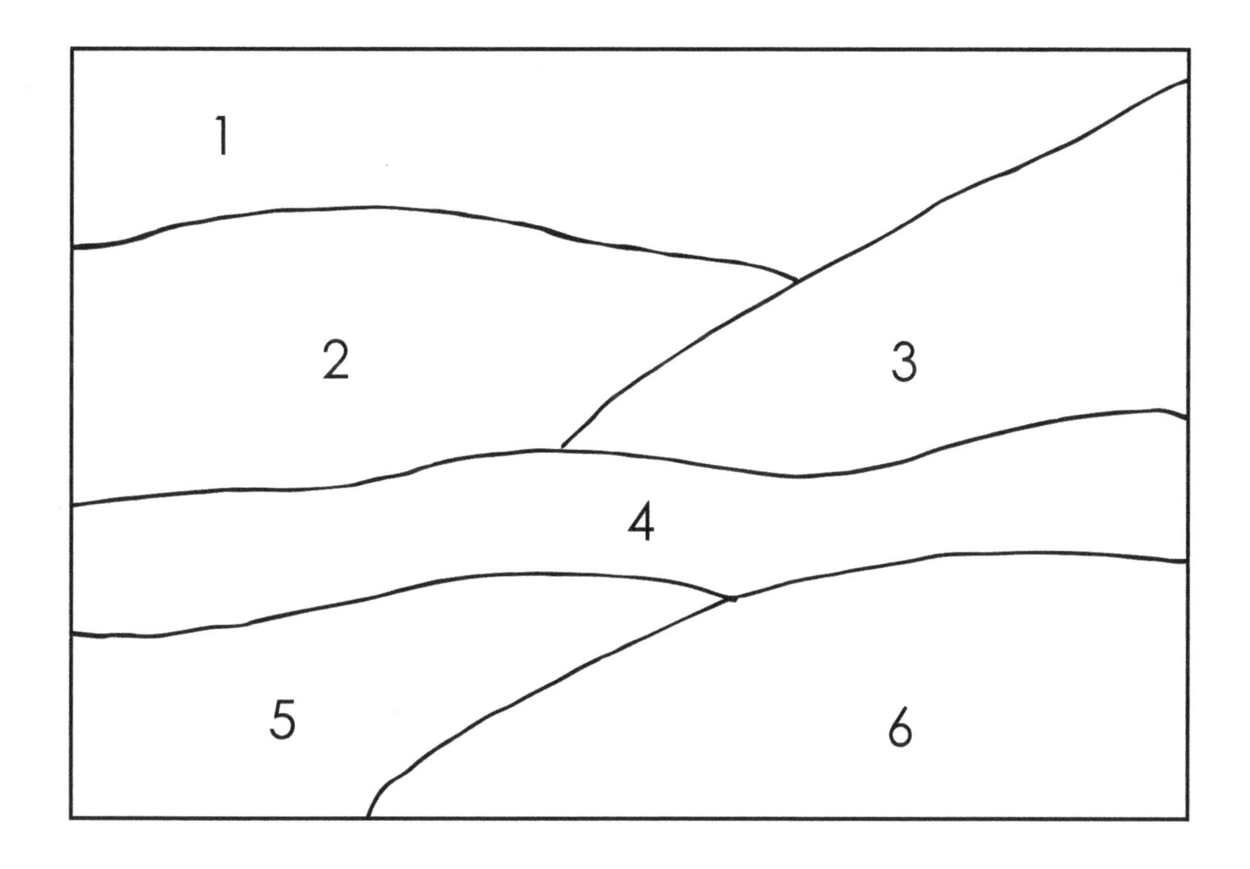

Vintage Sewing Machine

 - Expert

However much I love my modern sewing machines, there is just something romantic and beautiful about the old black hand sewing machines, their shape and many have lovely decoration.

I made my first quilt using my Mother's old hand Singer machine (which she received as an 18th birthday present in 1950) and I still have it and I won't get rid of it. It is the inspiration for this postcard and many other bits I have made.

This postcard is a great one for any sewing friends or lovers of vintage.

You will need to make this postcard

- 2 pieces of white cotton fabric 4½" x 6½"
- 2 pieces of iron-on interfacing 4½" x 6½"
- 1 piece of wadding 4" x 6"
- Fusible web
- A selection of fabrics
- A selection of sewing threads
- Stranded embroidery cotton
- Micron Pigma Pen
- Fabric paint and a very fine paint brush

1) Draw the Base and Main Body onto the paper side of the fusible web and cut out with a ¼" extra all round.

2) Press onto the chosen fabrics and cut out on the line.

3) Press the design pieces onto the prepared background fabric.

4) Layer with the wadding and rectangle of white fabric.

5) Machine stitch the design.

It can be a bit fiddly to do but I prefer to stitch this card in a narrow zig-zag. Remember to straight stitch the frame.

6) Embroider on the needle and handle.

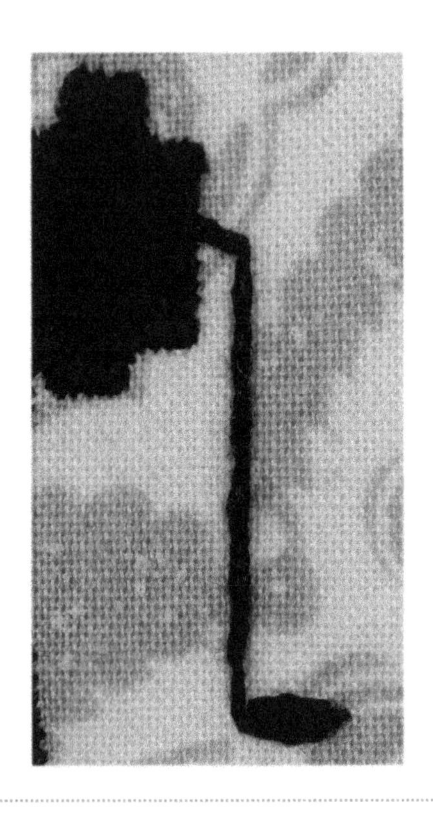

7) Draw on the stick for the thread reel using the Pigma pen.

8) Paint the decoration on the body of the machine and once the paint has dried, press to set the paint.

9) Pin the stabilised white fabric rectangle on the back and stitch around a number of times.

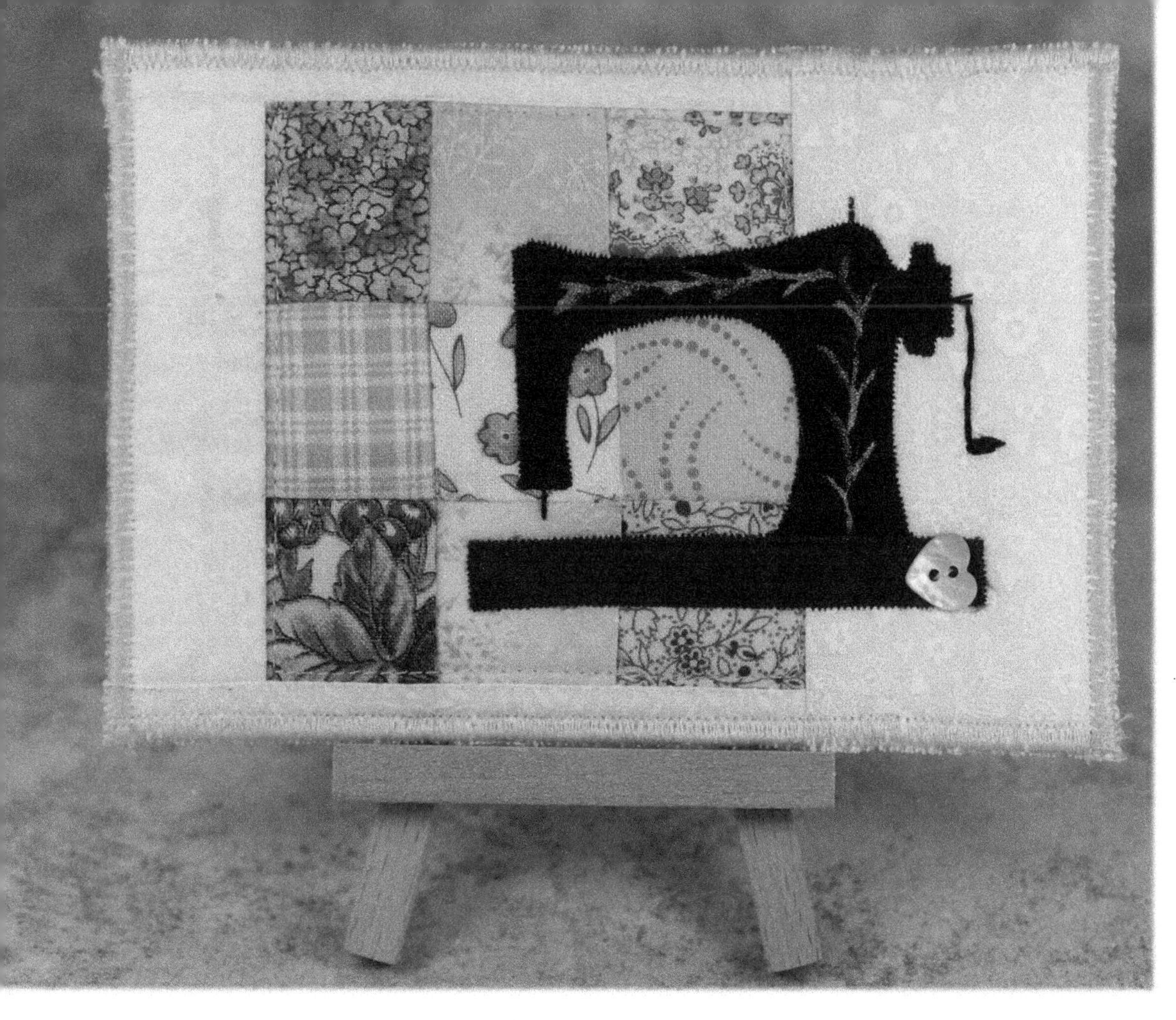

For a friend who loves patchwork, I have pieced a nine patch block as the background using 1½" squares and added a heart button.

For someone who loves sewing then a cotton reel adds interest and if you know their favourite colour then the thread can be in that colour.

This has more of a vintage feel, with scraps of ribbons and embroidery with a heart button.

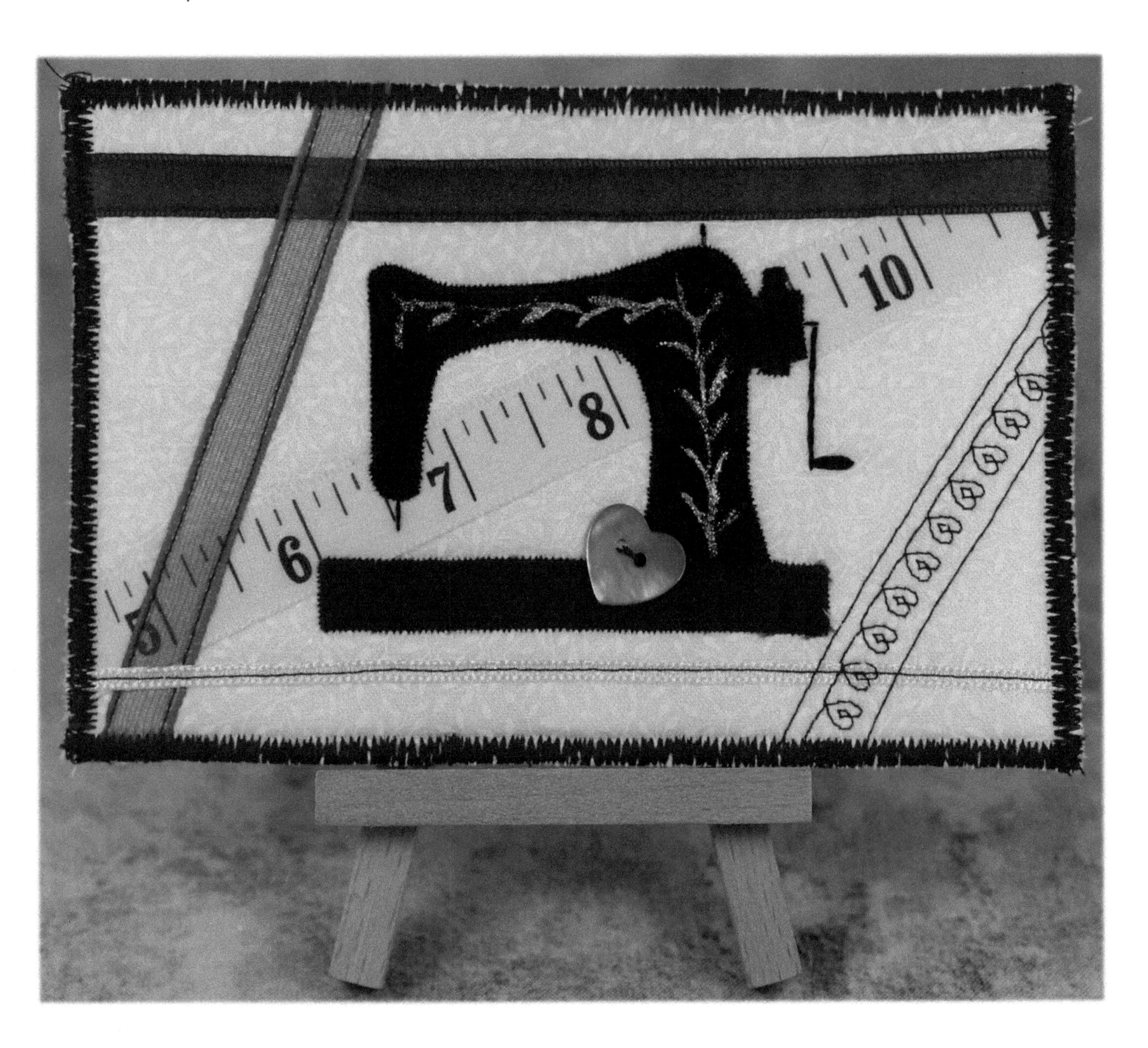

As well as scraps of ribbons, you can use scraps of lace, more buttons and embroidery or even clean old lace, or an embroidered hankie as details.

Template for Vintage Sewing Machine

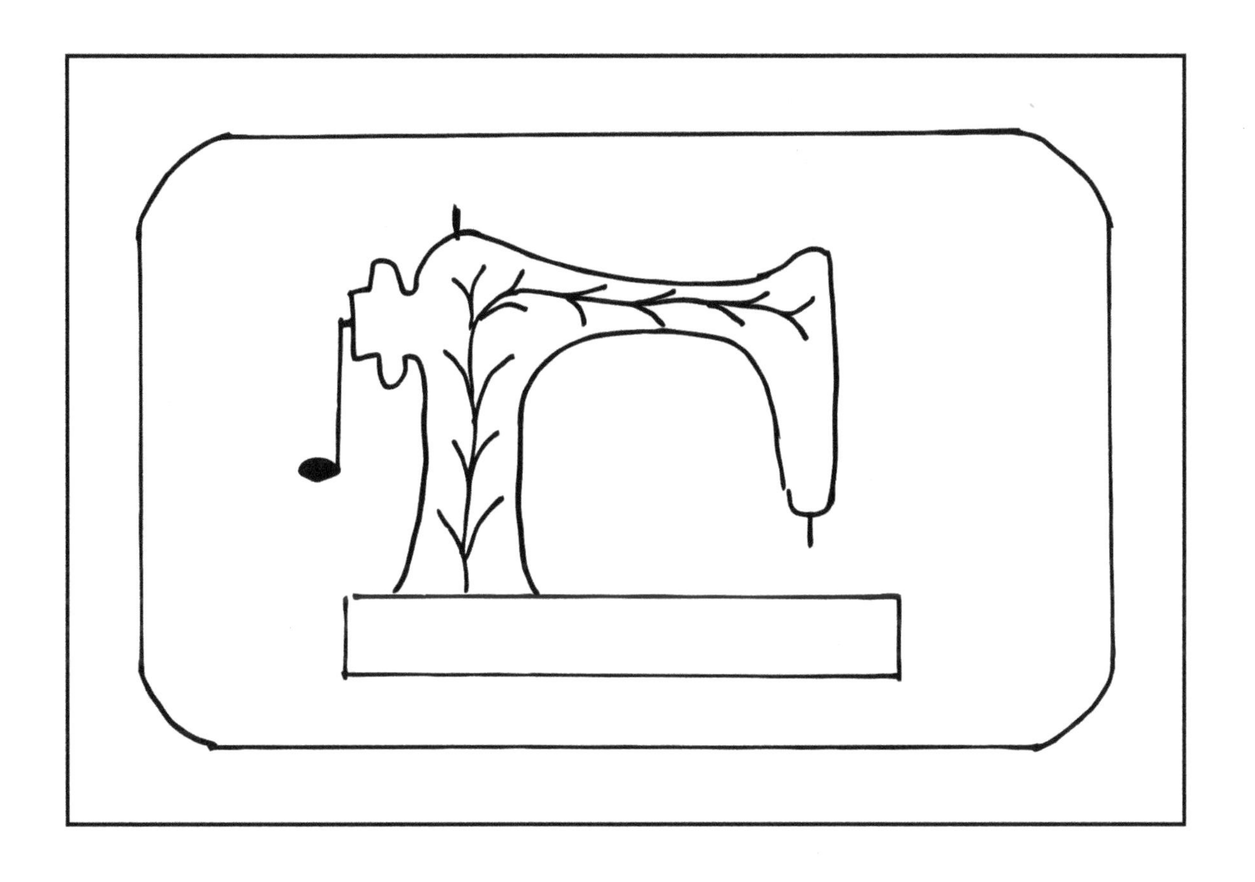

Extra Templates for Vintage Sewing Machine

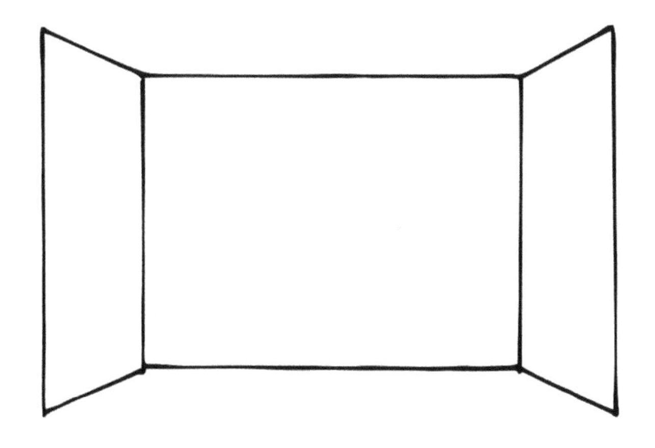

Presentation Card

When I first started making the Quilted Postcards I would just put them in an envelope and send them or give them to the recipient. But I was never happy with this presentation as they didn't feel properly finished.

I had lots of blank cards and paper and card from when I made paper-based cards, so I played around with different ways of mounting them. I was never really happy until one day, as I was going through a very old photo album with the photos mounted using corner tabs, I had a light bulb moment!

You will need to make this presentation card

- A5 blank card and matching envelope
- A5 piece of patterned backing paper
- 11cm x 16cm piece of firm card
- 4 pieces 2cm x 4cm in same firm card
- Double sided sticky tape
- Sellotape
- Scissors
- Scoring tool (option)

As all my paper crafting cutters are in metric and I always demonstrated in metric for the card making, the measurements for this presentation card are in metric – all my patchwork is worked in imperial!

1) Put double sided sticky tape on the back of the piece of A5 backing paper.

2) Peel off the paper strips and stick onto the front of the A5 blank card.

3) Take the 11cm x 16cm piece of card and place it right side down on the table, stick double sided sticky tape on the corners.

I use card of about 220gsm weight.

4) Working on one corner at a time, take a 2cm x 4cm piece of card and slip it behind the first corner, right side down, so it lays diagonally across the corner. This piece creates the corner mount.

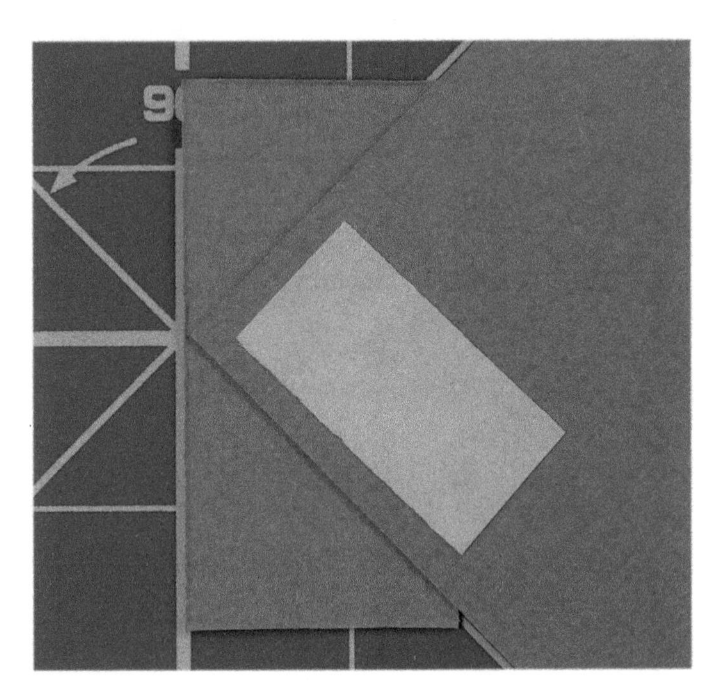

5) On the corner mount strip score lines.

I you don't have a scoring tool then the tip of a Biro works just as well.

6) Fold the scored lines.

7) Remove the paper from the double sided sticky tape on the 11cm x 16cm card and stick the corner mount down. Cut a small piece of Sellotape and stick over the corner mount. Work all four corners in the same way.

The reason I stick a piece of Sellotape over the corner mount is, I have found over the years, that occasionally the corner mounts pop open and by putting the Sellotape over them, they stay attached and flat better.

Yes, my Sellotape is gold! The only time I buy a new big reel of Sellotape to go on the big dispenser is Christmas and they always have a free small reel of gold in the pack. I put these in my craft drawer under my work desk and so when I am doing anything that needs Sellotape they are to hand and I don't have to run downstairs to get the big dispenser.

8) Put double sided sticky tape on the back of the 11cm x 16cm card.

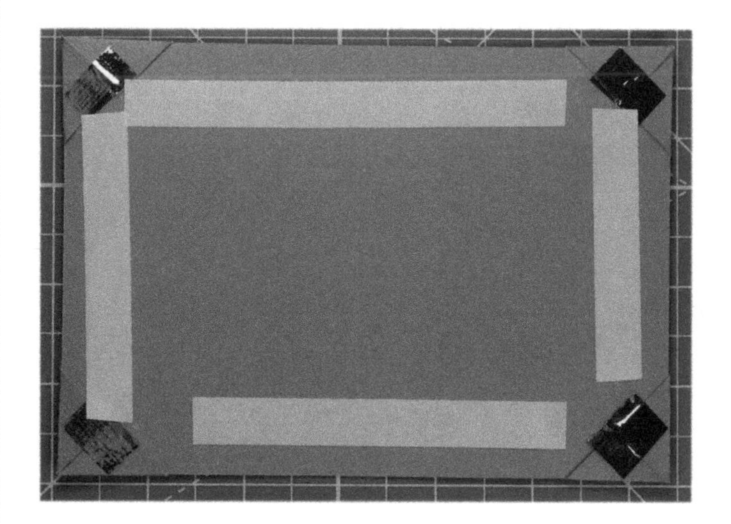

9) Peel off the backing paper and stick centrally onto the front of the card.

The card can be portrait or landscape and the corners of the Quilted Postcard just slip into the corner mounts and it is held in place. I regularly use peel off stickers to add messages or corner details to my cards.

Embroidery Stitches

I mainly use three proper embroidery stitches, for the details. I do also use random different length stitches for things like grass or to add texture. I have given basic instructions for Split Stitch, French knot and Lazy Daisy stitch but like everything else in this book, it is only what I use, please use whatever stitches you want to.

French Knot

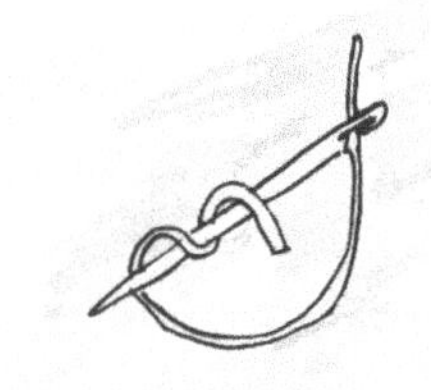

1) Bring the threaded needle up where you want the French knot to be.

2) Hold the needle horizontal to the fabric and wrap the thread round the needle, two or three times, holding the thread taut.

3) Insert the needle through the fabric, right next to where it came out, keeping the thread taut and pull the needle through the fabric to form the knot.

I have seen different ways to stitch a French Knot but I have shown the way I use. I will admit that French knots take practice to get right!!

The number of times I wrap the thread round the needle, depends on the look I am trying to get, twice round creates a smaller knot, three times a bigger one. By holding the thread taut as I pull the needle through gives a tight knot, if you want a baggier knot don't hold it taut. And finally I don't go back down the hole the thread comes out, as it is more likely for the knot to disappear and slip to the back!!! I insert the needle just next to it.

Split Stitch

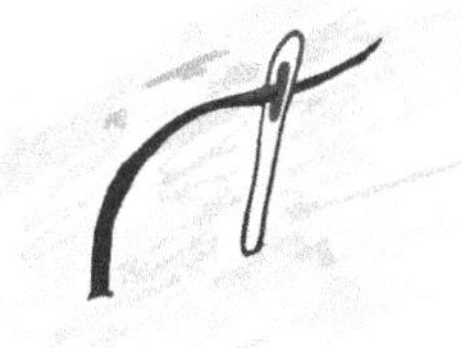

1) Bring the threaded needle up to the front of the fabric at the start of the line to be stitched and create one basic stitch.

2) Then bring the needle back through to the front of the fabric a third of the way down the first stitch, 'splitting' the thread.

3) Take the needle to the back of the fabric to finish the stitch. Continue creating stitches in this way.

I prefer the look of this stitch rather than the more common Back Stitch. The other stitch that is similar in look to Split Stitch is Stem Stitch

By changing the length of your stitch you can create a smooth line, so going round curves or circles I will use smaller stitches than on a straight line.

Lazy Daisy Stitch

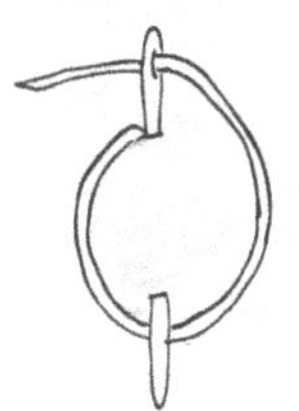

1) Bring the threaded needle up where you want the stitch to start. Take it back down right next to it, but don't pull the eye through.

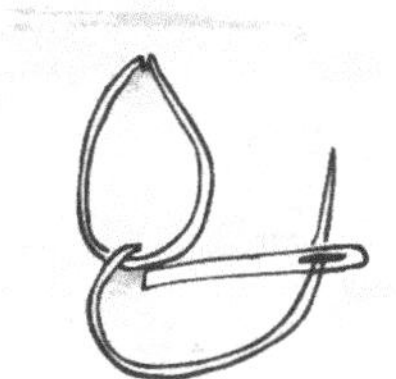

2) Bring the needle back up where you want the stitch to finish making sure the thread is sandwiched between the point of the needle and the fabric.

3) Pull the thread to form a loop.

4) Bring the needle down the other side of the thread, creating a small holding stitch.

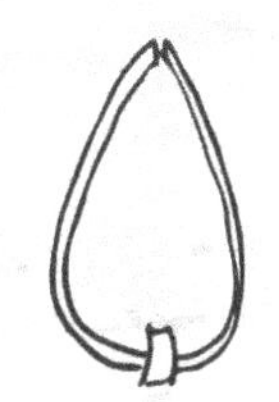

Lazy Daisy Stitch is a single unit of Chain Stitch and is really good for flower petals.

About Me!

Since I was nineteen-years-old I have been addicted to patchwork quilting after I went to The National Patchwork Championship, just to fill the coach that was going. The Quilted Postcards are just part of the creativity that surrounds me. I have been teaching Patchwork and Quilting for a long time, in recent years at my local Arts Centre and I have had some of my designs published in magazines.

I made my first Quilted Postcard in 2008. I saw an article on creating postcards with pre-printed fabric and at that time I was trying to find something to replace the ties I had been making for my husband Tony. For about 15 years I had been making mad, loud ties for Tony for birthdays, Christmases and any other time I wanted to give him a gift. He was known at his work for his ties (and yes he wore them everyday). Then the company decided that the engineers had to wear logo-ed polo shirts and I no longer had something to make for him.

The idea of Quilted Postcards really appealed to me and so I began creating them, first of all using the designs from the ties – just for Tony. Then our daughter Laura decided she liked them and from there it has spread to family and friends. I used to make over a hundred a year but I've recently cut back to only 80 or so!! I make them for birthdays, Christmases, Easter, and just as a personal gift. Or, if you are Laura, one 'Yellow Duck' postcard a month until she turned 18 and I ran out of ideas.

The Tortoise Logo

As a child on holiday in Yorkshire, I can remember going to a museum/workshop of a furniture maker. He carved a mouse into all his creations. That man was Robert Thompson. The idea of a having an animal on everything to identify it has always stayed with me.

When I was looking for a logo to 'stamp' on my postcards, using the tortoise just felt right. It had been a long running joke between Tony and I that I was happy to stay safely in my shell/home. I drew up my tortoise logo – no plain, normal shell but a patchwork of colours with a scarf – I do love scarves – and carrying a bag of knitting – something else I do, along with crochet and weaving. The tortoise is me.